Carrying the Banner

Jean Salter Roetter

Published by Compass Flower Press

an imprint of AKA-Publishing

ISBN 978-1-936688-96-8 Hardback

Also available in Trade Paperback: ISBN 978-1-936688-97-5

This book is dedicated to my mother,
Katharine Shepard Hayden Salter,
and my grandfather,
Harry Johnson Hayden III

ACKNOWLEDGMENTS

My sister Pat and brother Kit were both wonderful in helping me get my manuscript from "rough stage" to "clean copy." Pat took the rough copy, and edited out spelling errors, misplaced commas and awkward sentences. She brought great enthusiasm to the project along with her expertise.

Brother Kit squeezed hours out of his thirty-hour days to make it press-ready. I am grateful to each of them for their important contributions.

I also want to thank my sister Kate for her never-ending belief in this work. I would like to thank Yolanda Ciolli for creating the lovely banner graphic as well.

—Jean Salter Roetter
Summer 2014

i

RECOLLECTIONS

"How dear to this heart are the scenes of my childhood,
When fond recollection present them to view."

"The Old Oaken Bucket"
Samuel Woodworth (1817)

I didn't realize when I was a child what a magic circle of time I was in. It was only when childhood was over, and I looked back from a vastly changed perspective that I realized what I had been through. Although I am not really conscious of when my childhood began, I do know when I was in it, and I believe I know when it came to an end. And it is this in-between time that calls forth such lovely recollections and caused me to write this book.

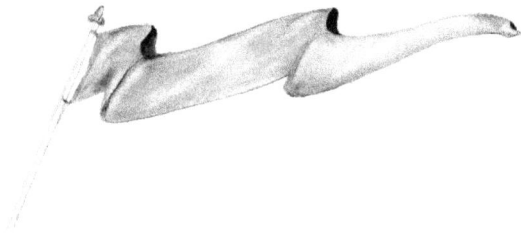

CARRYING THE BANNER

CHAPTER ONE

I have often wondered if our family would have known half the fun we experienced if we had ever had enough money. My mother, so full of imagination and fantasy and memories, led us to many different spots, always with the hope that we would save money by changing locations. The places she took us always reflected some wonderful experience from her own youth—the "scenes from [her] childhood." Her childhood had been safe and secure. However, from the time she married my father, things were different. Although her life had many different facets—freedom, independence (women's lib was never an issue in our lives because we were liberated from the beginning), there was one facet it did not possess—financial ease. Dockie—that's what we called our father—was an assistant professor at the

University of Wisconsin when Mother planned our "golden sojourn" in Berea, Kentucky.

My father was not a traditional daddy. Small children did not particularly interest him, so he was probably relieved to be left behind in some simple abode when, in 1933, Mother decided to take me, my two sisters and my brother off to Berea, Kentucky, to "save money." Why Berea? Because, after earning her Master's degree in English from Oberlin College, she had taught for one year at Berea College and had been very happy there. As our family was always broke and moving from one rented house to another, Mother came up with the idea that if we went to Berea and lived, say, in an inn (and she knew of a wonderful one right on the Dixie Highway), we could save money on house rent, utilities, heat—everything. The fact that we would be moving all that distance and maintaining two households did not dampen her enthusiasm. The idea was greeted with equal optimism by my equally impractical father, and move to Kentucky we did!

Oh, what excitement we felt as we approached the great white inn, Villawood Inn in Berea, Kentucky. We saw it set back from the highway, surrounded by tall trees and woods, and a handsome grove of thick green bushes. This large, gleaming white, colonial-style dwelling would actually be our home! Kate, eleven, Pat, ten, Joel, seven, and I, nine, looked at each other in wild disbelief as we walked through the front door and bounded up to our quarters. Never had anything looked more inviting to us than our snug room with its Ben Franklin stove in the center, its old-fashioned rockers and spare chairs, and the enticing sleeping porch, which opened off of the central room.

It was evident that we were going to have Mother all to ourselves. When five people are confined to one room, there is no getting away from one another. Nor did we want to. We all loved each other greatly, and we adored our mother. Somehow we never got quite enough of her. She was a poet and musician, a lady so full of rich sensibilities that, give as she did and try as she would to be just a mother, she was always pulled by the call of her other pressing talents. This opportunity to have no door to close between her and us was a thrilling new experience.

It must have been pretty exciting for Mother too, because now she was not only in the beloved environment of yesteryear, she was freed of cooking responsibilities, since we would of course eat in the downstairs dining room. One can imagine how much money we were going to save in this venture, but never mind that. We had such fun together, had so many good jokes and were so proud of each other, that we felt nothing but great good cheer.

We had come to an inn owned by a very simple family. There was a time when we would have called them "hillbillies," but I am sure I would be dubbed intolerant for using such a designation today. Let me revert to "backwoods" family for safety's sake. The Jenkins, through some quirk of fate, had come into a fortune of $75,000, and with this great sum of money had purchased the beautiful, elegant Villawood Inn that was to be our home for a season. The only problem for the Jenkins themselves was that they had spent all of their money to purchase the Inn.

Now there was nothing left. The entire family—nine in all—was forced to live crowded into two rooms in the basement, while the upstairs rooms served to generate income. One might ask whether this family had moved up in the world—or down.

It didn't matter to us, because two of the Jenkins children were near our age—Bugs, a boy of thirteen, and his sister Alice, ten. They seemed like interesting new friends with their strange twanging Southern accent and almost primitive speech patterns. I remember the vigorous arguments I had with Alice over the pronunciation of "Mrs." She insisted that it be pronounced "Mizriz" because, as far as she was concerned, that is the way it was spelled. She unfailingly referred to Mother as "Mizriz Salter."

Another person in this inn was a marvelous black man named Frank, the cook. He always wore a little black silk stocking cap, which of course fulfilled sanitary requirements. For us, however, not knowing why he wore this cap, it made a striking impression. We had never before seen a man wearing a tight black silk cap, and we liked the sight. We liked the food he cooked too—all except the hominy. I can still remember that sticky, solid, cereal-like substance that appeared at every meal. We were old-fashioned children, which means that we didn't shout our disapproval of food we didn't like; we ate what was set before us. Everything else was tasty and forgotten by now, but not that vividly remembered hominy. Could there be a moral in this?

As for Mother, she must have rejoiced in having someone else do the cooking. Her strength was limited, and her interest in cooking only marginal. Even in earlier years with the help of a live-in student as an aide, or sometimes a person hired by Granddad as a maid, meals had never been a regular event in our house. The food was always good, but there was many an evening when we had what we called a "pick-up supper." So the experience of regular meals was an event in itself, which we all loved. But it is not just the memory of the regular meals, or the fun we had living in that snug room that infuses me with such a warm and loving feeling; it is actually the fullness and diversity of the experiences we had in that one brief year.

For example, Kate and Pat discovered, after less than a week in their new school, that they knew more English grammar than their teacher. They persuaded Mother, after a few vivid descriptions of wild shouting and slapping episodes from the schoolroom, that they could learn more at home than in this particular freewheeling schoolroom. The combination of a complete set of Compton's Encyclopedia and Mother's infinite fund of knowledge was to be pitted against a backwoods school setting where only the most rudimentary skills and information were dispensed, under the aegis of a rough and tough young woman. Many of the students came from primitive pockets of isolated families living in the surrounding hills. The teacher and these students were well matched because they understood each other. Kate and Pat, coming from so different a background, family, and school, were definite misfits. Their wishes prevailed. Mother succumbed to the persuasive demands of her two eloquent older daughters.

Oh, how I envied them! And how I tried to persuade Mother that my teacher, a Mrs. Rice, was also unworthy. But alas, I was unsuccessful. Mrs. Rice was perfectly worthy, and Mother knew it. I couldn't come up with even one horror story to support my plea. Actually, what I remember about Mrs. Rice after all these years is that she wore the same dress—a black silk emblazoned with gigantic red and green flowers—every day of the school year. I recognize this as a sign of poverty now, which was so prevalent in that small Kentucky hill town, but then, I thought it was surely a matter of choice. In my memory, there remains too a little girl named Rowena who came to school without shoes—because she had no shoes. Rowena was a pretty girl, and she was dear to my heart because she gave me my very first May basket!

In addition to the fact that Kate and Pat seemed always to be on vacation—they observed not only the public school holidays, but several of their own, which they would designate as the spirit moved them—the hardest thing for me to accept about going to school while they did not was their "classroom." It consisted of a giant oak, full of ample branches that stretched and wound as far as the eye could see, with ladder-like limbs laden with dense green leaves. It made a perfect study spot, and it was here that I often found my two fortunate sisters when I roller-skated in from school. Here in this mighty tree, which we named "Monkey Jump," Kate and Pat perched high above the ground, comfortably settled on a lofty branch. In the sweet air, up amongst the melodious sounds of the singing birds, they read their lessons and prepared their "topics" and considered the merits of home schooling. Meanwhile, Joel and I dutifully and reluctantly attended the public school.

Another great memory connected to school in that period was my intense passion for roller-skating. I roller-skated to and from school with such vigor that, by the end of the school year, I was down to the ball bearings. It is hard to believe now, when I try my hand at skating, that I was ever such a passionate and able skater. I felt about skates the way Toad in *The Wind in the Willows* felt when he first discovered cars.

It isn't school, however, that occupies my thoughts the most when I reminisce about Berea. There were other wonderful things: the Star Players, the Estill Street Ramblers, Needle Eye Cave, and the Georgia Hillbillies.

The Star Players—what a group we were. There were five of us: Kate, Pat, a friend by the name of Alice Weeks, another friend named Cherry Churchill, and myself. We rather cleverly (we thought) called ourselves the Star Players in order to represent the five points of a star.

Alice had an actual little house in her backyard, and that house had a stage in it. It was the sight of this stage, which got our dramatic juices flowing, and dramatic juices we had a-plenty! Alice, who was eleven, and Cherry, who was ten, were not accustomed to the kind of creative endeavors that were a regular part of our daily life. Because we had been blessed with a mother who never said she was too busy when we announced that we had a show to put on, we had grown up putting on shows, which consisted of dancing, singing, declaiming, and acting. But never had we had a stage to work with. So now, in the summer when other kids were wondering what to do with themselves, we, the Star Players, readied ourselves for our newly created Sunday night series.

Kate was our leader, and she wrote all the plays. Whatever thrilled and excited an audience was subject matter for her deft and inexhaustible pen. She wrote of danger, of ghosts and dying crones, of desperation in many forms. We emoted and wept and moaned with passion and energy. Our audience was nearly as enthusiastic as we, and gladly paid the cost of admission: five cents a show. We sold both season and individual tickets, and we really sold them. I can still see the slim, white piece of paper that served as a ticket; and I can remember, too, the excitement we felt at earning real money as a result of our strenuous and dedicated labor on the stage of Alice Weeks' little playhouse.

What pleasure those Sunday nights held for us all! The little house was large enough to accommodate not only the parents of each of the Star Players, but our friends as well. There we gathered, and created theater without really knowing what a marvelous thing it was to be actually writing, producing, and acting in an original play every week. We loved the entire package, from concept to performance.

Summer was wonderful in Berea. The days were mellow and filled with the songs of crickets, hot sunshine, warm breezes, and sweet smells. When we weren't climbing Monkey Jump, we often sat on an old stile that divided the fairgrounds near Villawood Inn from the grove next to the Inn. Bugs Jenkins, Alice Jenkins, handsome Tom Vaughn, Kate, Pat and I, and a few others whose faces and names I no longer remember, formed another group. We called ourselves the Estill Street Ramblers. Our purpose was to make music. Handsome Tom—he of the Greek-statue-like features and blond wavy hair—played the guitar, Bugs, the ukulele, and the rest of us sang. We sat on the stile on those lazy summer afternoons and, as the guitar was strummed and the ukulele twanged, we sang cowboy songs. This is known as country western today, but for us, it was cowboy music.

In 1934, there was no finer exponent of this kind of music than a spirited quartet called the "Georgia Hillbillies," who held forth on the radio every morning at seven-thirty. They announced their radio presence with a frenzied rendition of the old favorite, "Nola." After that wonderful song heralding their presence, they proceeded to play guitar and sing about the lonesome life of a range rider. We had our own favorite ballad which told about a lonely cowboy "with a heart so brave and true, who learned to love a lady with eyes of heavenly blue," lyrics that sang to us of the life of a cowboy. As we sang this sad song, and others like it, it was as if we had grown up on the plains of Montana, we were so full of sorrow and mournful tones.

We were filled with curiosity and a desire for change and excitement. We looked for a variety of ways to fill our days. Towards that end, one day we decided to undertake an exploration of a cave we had heard about, called Needle Eye Cave. It was located in the foothills of the mountains surrounding Berea. The Ramblers set out in mid-morning with a tasty picnic lunch and a lot of determination to explore this mysterious-sounding cave, which we had heard was dark and scary and filled with "cave-like" things.

We reached the cave around lunchtime. It was a hot summer day, quiet, with only the sound of cowbells coming from a nearby meadow. Uncertain about what it would actually be like to crawl into a cave, we decided to eat our lunch before beginning the exploration. When we were all ready, Bugs stuck his head into the cave. Much to our dismay, he discovered it was pitch black. We hadn't counted on this. Undaunted, we solved the problem by building a small fire and finding sticks that would serve as torches. This gave a special jolt of excitement to the project.

The cave entrance was small. We could enter only one by one. We decided that the oldest would lead the way. I was very glad to be one of the younger ones, one of those in the background, for the cave appeared very cold and very black. And black it would stay, because there wasn't enough good air to keep the torches burning, and the leaders kept returning for a relight. Finally, Pat announced that she wasn't going to bother with a torch but would make her way forward by feeling. And what a feel it was—cold, clammy and moist! We moved forward very slowly, ever more slowly, because we found that it was one thing to plan an exploration of this sort, but quite another to actually execute it.

Finally, someone asked in a quavering voice, "How much more is there?" All our torches were out. Pat, who knew how one of our favorites—Nancy Drew—might handle such a situation, said she would toss a rock out and see if it would tell us anything. Pat threw the rock, and we heard a faint splash from far, far below. But for that rock and that splash, we might all have gone down into the great pit we now knew was dead ahead. What a lucky throw!

We turned around and swiftly got ourselves out of the darkness and back into the sunshine. How lovely the warm air felt—it was like an embrace. The sound of the cowbells—those wonderful cowbells—was like music; it connected us with the comforting, safe outside world. We left the cold, cheerless world of the cave and the watery pit behind us joyfully and gratefully and headed home.

On another occasion we decided that we wanted to go on a camping trip. We prevailed upon Mr. Weeks, Alice's father, to go with us on an overnight outing. Of course, since automobiles were very much a rarity in Berea, we knew we would be the beasts of burden. That didn't bother us! We assembled almost every available blanket, pillow, pot and pan, and food item we could gather, loaded ourselves up, arms full to overflowing with all of these goods, and in joyous spirits set forth towards a spot about two miles outside of town. We loved the going. To us, it seemed romantic to be walking through the small glades of trees, along the back roads that led us to our destination.

A little before sundown, we arrived at a secluded spot near the edge of a pleasant country field. We made our beds from the pillows and blankets, which we had carried so diligently, and then, set about preparing a light supper. Everything tasted very good and spirits were high, even though we had spied some thickening gray clouds overhead, and had heard a few distant rumblings that sounded very much like thunder.

When we were all settled for the night in our snug blankets, those clouds and rumbles turned into something big and real, loud and wet. The pitch black of the night was illuminated by great flashes of zigging and zagging bolts of lightning. Rain gushed down in waterfall-like torrents. We were in the middle of something very wet and, to paraphrase an old gospel song, "there warn't no hiding place down there!" There was no place for us to go for shelter. The lightning was too intense for us to consider going under any tree. So there was nothing to do but to stumble around in the dark, and gather up all of our belongings so that we could make our way home.

We had no flashlight. The blankets and pillows, which had been heavy and awkward to carry when dry, were now wet and soggy, and weighed many times their original weight. The pots and pans, too, were worse now than in the beginning because they were somewhat dirty and slippery. What a trek we had back to town! How different the trees looked as we made our way in the dark, and tried to avoid being under one when the lightning struck. I imagine that the conscientious Mr. Weeks asked himself just how he had gotten himself into the position of being shepherd and guide for a bunch of strenuous young people on a rainy night like this one!

We reached town about midnight, and headed directly for the Weeks's home. The pleasure of opening a door and going inside where it was warm, dry, and light can easily be imagined. Once more we made up our beds and lay down for the night. Only this time, we were able to sleep through the night. By morning, our adventure had taken on its own glow. All the remembered difficulties seemed greatly diminished as we marveled at our ability to handle adversity.

When I marshal my memories, many come surging up. I think of the hot summer afternoon when Bugs, Kate, Pat, Tom, and I were all climbing Monkey Jump. We three sisters had found a perch midway up the mighty oak, but Bugs and Tom were not satisfied with so accessible a spot. They both climbed higher, ever higher, where the branches grew slimmer and seemed less secure. They found a branch at the top of the tree, and there they paused. As we looked up at them, we felt slightly uneasy because they were very high up, and it didn't look safe.

Suddenly, there was a great crackling sound and, to our horror, as we followed our ears with our eyes, we saw Bugs and Tom falling—pitching down through the air, as though they had been tossed by some giant hand. Their branch had broken and they were on their way down. Watching them fall was a terrifying experience. We felt utterly helpless. There was nothing we could do.

Bugs' fall was suddenly interrupted. His new, shiny stiff pants caught on a branch and held him by the tear in his trousers. But poor Tom had no such luck, and down he went to the ground beneath us, where he lay at the foot of the oak, still and broken. When the ambulance arrived, we learned that both his legs had been fractured. We watched from the tree frozen, as the paramedics rushed over to his motionless body and took care of him. We simply couldn't move. Bugs wouldn't move for a totally different reason. He was embarrassed because of the tear in his pants!

That was the last time any of us ever climbed Monkey Jump. For a long time we didn't even want to look at our beloved tree. It never seemed the same again. Nor did Tom. Although his legs healed, his sweet, friendly nature was somehow altered by the attention he received in the hospital, and we all felt that he had become spoiled.

Then there was the time that I went to see Frank's baby—Frank of the black silk cap, the cook at the Inn. I remember this visit because it was such a steaming summer day outside, and so hot inside the little shack where Frank and his wife lived.

The little one-room dwelling near the Inn had about five windows. Each was tightly closed with shades completely drawn. Not a breath of fresh air pierced the interior of the room. The small baby lay dressed in a sweater, and was wrapped in blankets in this suffocating room.

It was the first time I had ever been in the home of a black family or had seen a black baby. Even the excitement of actually being in Frank's house, and seeing his cute little baby covered with prickly heat, could not hold me. I needed to get away from that dark, hot room, and back to fresh air and soft breezes. And yet how proud that mother was of her baby, and how carefully she saw to it that it was covered at all times as she showed off her prize! In retrospect, I think of how often mothers do so carefully for their children what they think is best, and alas, how often they are mistaken. It is wonderful that we all survive each other's good intentions.

Speaking of good intentions, Mother's intentions for the family bank account had certainly produced a marvelous year for us, but I doubt there was one extra dollar in the bank. In spite of our concentrated pleasure during that wonderful year in Berea, no one seemed to mind when the time came to go home. We all approached the prospect of the train trip from Lexington, Kentucky to Madison, via Cincinnati with great delight. We were going to take an all-night excursion coach. This meant, of course, that we would be sitting up rather than lying comfortably in a Pullman berth. Mother had a delightful capacity for putting things into a perspective that turned what could have been a hard time into a lark. And she did this with the homeward trip. We called our mode of travel "carrying the banner." I am still not quite sure how we arrived at that phrase, but we did so, and the phrase infused all of us with a sense of purpose and excitement as we readied for takeoff.

Somehow, in the course of the past year, our belongings had increased and our suitcases had not, so we were faced at the end with some extra things for which there was no suitable place.

Perhaps this is where I first learned of the marvels of the brown paper shopping bag. Soon we all had shopping bags crammed with the "extras." And the extras in my case were pair upon pair of beloved roller skates. Each of us had our own pair, and they all wound up in bags. Along with the roller skates came some goodies to snack on during the trip, chiefly bananas and sandwiches.

We had a game plan: Pat and I were to hold the carryalls (and we did indeed make them live up to their name), and Mother, Kate, and Joel were to handle the other items that hadn't been checked ahead.

Everything went well on the trip from Lexington to Cincinnati. The train was comfortable, and it was still early enough in the day that no one was too sleepy. We had such fun on the train as it chugged through the lovely Kentucky countryside. But when we got to Cincinnati, the unexpected happened. We had all taken our designated bags and were dutifully following Mother from the arrival gate to the departure gate. However, because the departure gate happened to be on the other side of the station, we had to walk through the entire station. It was built in the style of stations of yesteryear—massive with abundant marble, dozens of benches, and plentiful space. Because the train was the most popular form of travel then, there were always many people sitting on the benches watching travelers come and go. There was, in fact, no better place in the world to people-watch than a busy train station.

We gave people something to watch that night. We had just about reached the center of the station when our brown paper carryalls began to give way. They crumpled and ripped and broke, and simply fell apart. Out popped the roller skates! One to the right, one to the left, three to the front, another to the rear, and all of them rolling and rolling fast. The bananas followed the skates out of the bag, so suddenly we had to make sure that we weren't skidding on a banana as we sought to retrieve a skate. No matter how fast we ran to catch the skates, they seemed to get away from us. And of course, when we did at last get the skates together again, we had no bags in which to put them because the bottoms had given out. We had no choice but to carry all of the skates in our arms—an almost impossible feat. And yet, somehow we managed to finally get to the train that was to take us the rest of the way. We got back to Madison on schedule, roller skates and all. From that day on, the family had a new phrase in their vocabulary. We knew that if ever we heard the words "carrying the banner," it was a signal that tough times lay ahead!

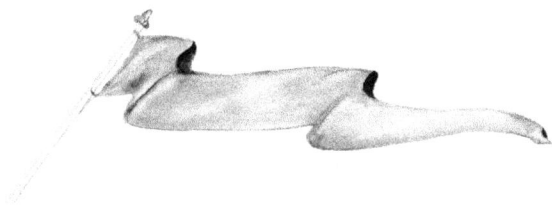

CHAPTER TWO

Getting back to Madison in 1934 meant a new home for us. This time it was an apartment in a court near Lake Mendota—a lake famous for being large, shapely, and sparkling clean. The apartment was spacious and comfortable, wonderful for us to roam in. It was located near the University campus, which was grand for my father.

Memories from Mendota Court days are fleeting and diffused. They are of summer days spent on the shores of the lake, where we swam in the cool, unpolluted water; of walks to school, kicking the leaves in autumn and making snowballs in winter; of playing new games (among them jacks) and making new friends—not knowing that one of my favorite jacks partners, John Bardeen, an older brother of a new friend, would turn out to be one of the inventors of the microchip!

Once again we formed a "gang," and this time our project was to put out a newspaper. We called it *The Mendota Court News.* We filled it with articles, news reports, features and even cartoons. A bright and lively boy named Johnny Meyers served as editor. We each had a specific job: writing the material, printing the paper, or delivering the finished product. This produced a wonderful sense of purpose and activity. Once again, our faithful, sympathetic parents accounted for the bulk of our readership, and willingly paid a nickel a copy for the privilege.

We also established a library among ourselves. We particularly liked this scheme because it enabled us to use a black-inked date stamp on blank sheets of paper that we inserted into small book pockets placed in each volume of our library. This was an innocent and most joyous occupation.

Unfortunately, not all of our activities were as mild as this one, and as a result we began to feel the confinement and difficulty of apartment living. Actually, I am amazed that we lasted as long as we did in the apartment, because of our own feelings and those of our neighbors. When I think of the zest with which Pat and I approached our lovely new Ping Pong table every day after school, I can only marvel that our downstairs neighbors survived as long as they did. And I marvel that we survived so long when I recall the sound of the typewriter used by the student living above us. He was a nocturnal typist, and his typing sounded as if horses were stamping and prancing overhead. So we had no recourse, really, except to move—but not, as we all enthusiastically agreed, into another apartment.

Because we had lived in a number of houses in Madison, we always referred to them by number rather than by the name of the street on which they were located. Our new dwelling then, which was on the west side of town, was known to us simply as 2103. The basic charm of this plain, square, two-toned black and orange house, with its modest front and back yards, was its large front porch from which we could survey the street. There apparently had not been any new kids on the block for a while, and our coming looked like an opportunity for some great fun.

Three neighbor boys—Don Feeney, Don Fellows, and Jimmy Macintosh—energetic, creative lads of our own age—decided to catch our attention in an unusual way. Shortly after our arrival in the new house, when Mother and Dockie were gone, these young gallants began to pelt us and our house with dirt balls. At first we weren't quite sure what to do about this unwanted attention. But after a brief period of cogitation and group discussion, we decided that there was nothing quite like water to douse enthusiasm. Without further ado, we took to throwing water from an upstairs window upon the heads of the eager young assailants.

It was a crazy way to start a friendship but it did indeed start one, in time. But first, there was the question of The Apology. I can still remember the smug pleasure we felt as the young men, one by one, came to our door to apologize for what they had done. Their mothers had learned of their welcome to us, and had taken immediate action. We smiled innocently as we stood next to Mother and listened as they delivered their apologies. The solemn words of repentance were uttered and accepted, and that was the end of it, paving the way for the birth of an inseparable sextet.

To say the words "Feeney, Fellows, and Macintosh" even to this day is almost like a mantra that conjures up images of laughter, summer idleness, companionship, and total devotion. Fellows was red-haired and freckled, Macintosh was blond and blue-eyed with an adorable Jimmy Stewart kind of grin, and Feeney was dark-haired and dark-eyed (sleepy eyes he had), and later was the object of an intense crush on the part of Pat. But during that first summer, it was just the six of us, constantly together, playing wonderful games like "Anagrams," "Go Fish," "I Doubt It," and then, at twilight or after an early supper, "Kick the Can" and "Run, Sheepie, Run!" until the darkness finally drove us all indoors and to bed.

That was also the summer of the mumps. Joel, Kate and Pat all got the mumps, and received all of the wonderful attention that went with being sick in my family. One of Mother's great experiences had been the six weeks she spent at the Vassar Training Camp for Nurses during World War I, and the latent image of herself as Florence Nightingale came to the fore whenever we were sick—which made being sick a pleasant experience in our household. But I, alas, did not catch the mumps that summer. All I got was a two-week quarantine for each case of mumps in the family. That made a total of six weeks in quarantine, during which time I was confined to the yard and house. I watched each sister and my brother get well and return to the outside world while I had to stay behind, ruing my misfortune at not getting the mumps. (Years later I felt the same regret, for when I finally got them, I was the mother of three small children, and could ill afford to be sick.)

Because we had moved so much, upon entering sixth grade, I had very few buddies connected with school. There was, however, a rather plump, quiet classmate by the name of Shirley. There was nothing about her that would have drawn me to her in normal circumstances. But these were not normal times. In sixth grade, you don't feel okay unless you have at least one buddy—a person you can walk to and from school with, a person who will pick you for her team when picking time comes.

Shirley was such a person for me, and I must have seemed so for her. She, too, was short of friends. She spied me as one who could provide the kind of necessary companionship we both longed for. We went everywhere together. Daily, we stopped on the way home from school at the ice cream stand where the newly invented soft-serve ice cream was sold. In any situation where a partner was required, we sought each other out. The fact that we had little to say to each other was not important. What mattered was that we had each other when having another person was essential. When my sisters looked askance and said to me (as they often did), "What do you see in Shirley?" I simply looked wise and said nothing. Shirley and I finally parted when we moved again, and I was enrolled in a new school. Happily for me, the sixth grade experience didn't repeat itself. Quite the contrary. I became president of my seventh grade class.

It is interesting to realize how little we are sometimes aware of what is going on right around us as it is actually happening. I am thinking specifically of the following year when Mother had a miscarriage. This in itself was not too bad, but it had severe consequences. Her doctor, who was also an "alleged" friend, decided to experiment with a new drug. He used Mother as his guinea pig. The experimental drug had the same effect on Mother as eight or ten cups of black coffee. The impact was dreadful. She couldn't sleep. Day after day she felt unwell. I knew she wasn't well because she spent most of her time in bed. This is what I mean when I say I knew and yet I didn't really know. My life continued in its merry course. I was so full of school activities and neighborhood happenings that I scarcely knew how awful things were for Mother. I've grown to think that children are more insulated from the trials that rage around them than we think.

Fortunately, even bad years come to an end, and this one did so at last. As the school year came to a close, there was change in the air. It was now 1937.

I had just finished seventh grade, and was enjoying the swing of life as we experienced it at Wisconsin High School, the high school associated with the University of Wisconsin. It was a school rich in fine teachers and programs that tapped the creative energies of its students. Whether we were in speech class performing for one another, on the debate team, in the school orchestra, on stage, or leading a school assembly; we, the students, were fully involved in school activities. To coin a phrase, we felt that we had the world by the tail, and that we could swing it any way we wished. Oh, the happy illusions of youth. We had them all.

This time we weren't happy when Mother came up with her latest plan for saving money. As a youngster, she had enjoyed marvelous summers in Cutchogue, Long Island, a small fishing village near the tip of Long Island's north fork. She remembered those wonderful days and the simplicity of life in that little hamlet. She realized too that she had become increasingly uneasy about the fast pace of life in Wisconsin High. In addition, she knew that her beloved father, our adored grandfather, was in need of a home base from which to make trips to New York City. These were all seen as compelling reasons for relocating once again.

Granddad had always been a grand influence in our lives. In retrospect, I can see that only because he was there were we, as a family, able to do the many wild and impractical things we did. Granddad, with his wonderfully merry, generous spirit, his love of fun, and his adoration for his eldest daughter, often paid the bills—bills which otherwise might have weighed our whole operation down; might indeed have sunk it altogether. He'd fume and he'd lecture; he would even scold. But he dearly loved his daughter, Katharine, and our family, if for no other reason than he was so necessary to us. When he came to our house, there were dozens of things for him to do. There were hooks to be put up, door knobs to be tightened, the basement to be cleaned, dark corners to be swept out and tidied, shelves to be straightened, even half-empty milk bottles in the refrigerator to be consolidated. He was "a place for everything and everything in its place" person. As such, he was incredibly helpful and useful in our home, where everyone seemed more bent on doing their own thing than keeping everything in "its place."

The first thing that Granddad usually did when he came for a visit was to change into overalls and descend to the basement, knowing it would badly need organizing, cleaning, and a general toning up. (An Aegean stable had nothing on our basement, with its coal-burning furnace!) We would hear him whistling as he went contentedly about his work, and we knew that he was happy because he felt needed. There was no "Father, sit down now and rest!" in our house. It was rather, "Father, here's a job for you." or, "Granddad, can you fix this for me?"

And thus, off to Long Island we were to go. Why should we not all settle in Cutchogue, live very simply, and save a great deal of money? Such a scheme would accomplish two worthy purposes: provide an economical place to live with minimum sophistication in the school setting (unlike the dazzling Wisconsin High), and it would provide a home for Granddad. Dockie could come to visit us during holidays and he could live very inexpensively himself while we were saving money in our simple Long Island dwelling. The plan was barely conceived before it became a reality. Not only was it decided that we would be moving to the East by the end of the school year, but to further intensify the excitement in my life, I was invited, along with Joel, to spend the summer at my aunt's camp in Ontario, Canada. All of this was so exciting that we felt a little dizzy by the end of the school term—dizzy and delighted at all the prospects which lay beckoning before us.

Joel and I readied for the marvelous adventure of going to camp in Canada. We were going to travel via an overnight ship on Lake Erie, in the company of relatives we hardly knew. We got to know them quite well on the trip! They seemed to us overly proper and quite stuffy, and yet I fear that my aunt had a greater shock in meeting me than I did in meeting her, for hers was a boys camp, and although there was a cabin set aside for her daughter and the daughters of the female counselors, these people all looked very young indeed. If there was one thing about me that was obvious, it was that I did not look like an twelve-year-old child. I was as innocent as an eight-year-old, and what I didn't know about life and love and the birds and bees would have filled volumes, but I looked as though I knew it all. It must have been quite a shock for Aunt Jessie to have such a buxom, well-developed girl arrive at her boys camp! It was, nonetheless, a delightful summer for me. Canoeing, portaging, picking blueberries, crafting, square dancing (and being the belle of the dance!), getting acquainted with deep pine forests, singing around a campfire, meeting lots of new people—and meeting them individually rather than just as part of a family—was a thrilling change from anything I had done before.

When the summer had ended, as Joel and I left Canada to go to our new home in Greenport, Long Island, we had great fun talking over our summer. As we traveled south to meet Mother, Kate, Pat and Granddad, little did we dream what a lovely part of our lives was about to begin!

CHAPTER THREE

Greenport is a small fishing village at the end of the north fork of Long Island. One of the oldest villages in New York state, it is situated on Peconic Bay, a body of water that flows eventually into the ocean. It forms the center around which the whole community pivots. When we arrived in 1937, the town was filled with beautiful old houses, with docks where ships—both large and small—were anchored, with busy, working shipyards, and always the smell of the sea and the feeling of open water. The sound of the foghorn, the call of the crying gulls, and the tangy scent of saltwater were constants in the Greenport scene. What a new world this was, and what an exciting one! Is there anything more powerful for an inland person than to meet the world of saltwater for the first time? To know only lakes is not, I discovered, to be really acquainted with water. To meet a seacoast is to meet a force that is truly elemental, and it is this that we felt close to in Greenport.

But it wasn't just being near saltwater that made our coming to Greenport so exciting. Perhaps above all, it was the house we found to live in. Never in our entire lives had we come even close to living in such a house as the one we now rented. In present-day Greenport, where the house still stands, it is known as "The Gingerbread House," because of the fancy and handsome trim all around its top; but in our day, it was referred to simply as the overflow house for The Townsend Manor Inn, which was Greenport's most fashionable inn.

The house was situated on a spacious plot of land right on the main street. The address was, in fact, 726 Main Street. Pale yellow, with shuttered windows and creamy white ornamentation, it was set back from the public sidewalk. A wonderful circular walk led from the public sidewalk to our wide, shady front veranda, and then out again on the other side. Our land ran into the yard of the Townsend Manor Inn on one side, and on the other side of the veranda was a driveway leading to a great barn in back. As we approached the barn for the first time, we were enchanted by the sight of a gazebo, and our excitement could hardly be contained when we discovered that there were not only a barn and a gazebo in the backyard, but a tennis court as well. Our very own tennis court, in our very own back yard. Then—and this perhaps was the grandest thing of all—we discovered that we had our own waterfront. The back yard went right down to an authentic salt marsh inlet. This house was right on the water. We needed only a dock and a boat to become a seafaring family.

With all the beauty and amplitude of such surroundings, we would have been content if the house had been a hovel, but it was as wonderful inside as its grounds were outside. And the house was not merely beautiful, it was enormous! Our very family, which had once lived in one room plus a sleeping porch, was now to be the proud occupants of a seventeen-room dwelling! This house was complete with not only a bedroom for each person, but it also had hitherto-unheard-of rooms, such as a spacious ballroom ornately and lavishly embellished with curlicues and figurines evocative of all the prim delights of the Victorian age. There were, in addition, a music room, two guest rooms, plus "regular" rooms as Joel called them, like a dining room and a living room. There was even a small extra room tucked away at the top of the back stairs where a little old lady named Mrs. Smith lived. The house boasted front stairs, back stairs, and side stairs, so that there was not only a wonderful sense of space and movement, but of mystery as well. What excitement prevailed as we explored our glorious new space.

It was extraordinary, but we were considered rich because we were able to afford the required rent for this home, which was by Greenport standards very high—all of forty dollars a month. In Madison, we could find nothing at all for forty dollars a month, even in 1937; but here we were, marvelously ensconced in a seventeen-room house complete with barn, tennis court, gazebo, and a private outlet to the sea—all for less than fifty dollars a month.

The moving van arrived with our furniture at just about the same time we did. One has to have moved long-distance to appreciate the particular excitement one feels when the van, so carefully packed at the other end, arrives at the new destination. The familiar faces of the moving men take on the look of long-lost friends, perhaps because one feels strange in the new environment so that anyone even slightly familiar looks good. Perhaps it is because they are the caretakers of one's precious worldly possessions. Whatever it is, I can still remember the wonderful feeling we experienced when the Greyhound moving truck rolled into our driveway, and the men jumped down from the cab, ready to unload.

Settling into the house was remarkably easy. Our furniture filled the space satisfactorily, except for the ballroom. This elegant forty by twenty foot room was simply too large to even consider trying to furnish. It became a great extra space, and was fun to have, but it was not really used except as an occasional overflow "camping" spot when there seemed to be too many bodies underfoot. It also made an ideal setting for those time-honored all-night talk-a-thons of the young known as slumber parties.

Settling into the house may have been easy, but settling into the town and the school was quite a different story. I don't think that a new family had moved into Greenport for a long, long time, and I am certain that a new family like our family had not been seen for an even longer time. Greenport was basically a fishing village of simple, hardy, fine fisher folk. Such were the people they knew and were comfortable with. Such were the kind of people they expected. There was no way they could understand what this pretty lady, with her four children and her distinguished-looking, white-haired father, were doing in the big overflow house. "Where was the husband?" they queried among themselves. "And what were these girls going to offer in the way of competition to the local high school females?" This question was much on the minds of our youthful classmates, who seemed to regard us as formidable rivals.

How well I remember arriving at school each morning. The high school was one of those massive yellow brick school buildings so common in the 1930s, and withal, so utterly lacking in architectural beauty or charm. There was a "girls side," and a "boys side." We of course went to the girls side, and because the doors did not open until eight-thirty, everyone stood outside waiting for the big double doors to swing open. Our fellow students stood in clusters, talking among themselves. Kate, Pat, and I walked to school. As we reached the long sidewalk leading to the double doors, first one, then another, and finally the whole lot of girls turned to watch us approach. This they did silently, having ceased all talking as we grew nearer. This silent inspection of the newcomers was to become a ritual that lasted as long as we attended Greenport High. In the beginning, when we didn't know anyone, it was a peculiar agony made bearable only by the strength we drew from each other. As we became acquainted, however, the penetrating stare-down became less painful to us since, in time, we gained a few friends whose faces showed up in the crowd and helped to lessen the terrible sense of separateness.

I remember my first day in the eighth grade when I, having finally made it through the forbidding double doors, was thrust by the energetic teacher to the front of the class, where I was presented to that sea of unknown and, to my eyes, hostile faces, as "the new Jeannie Salter." The teacher's intentions were good, but oh, how uncomfortable and alone I felt. And how I longed for the staunch support and comforting presence of Kate and Pat.

I did not know it then, but looking back, I know now that each move we made to a new and strange place developed in me a certain ease about meeting new people, which has stood me in good stead all of my life. And, of course, flux being the law of the universe, one need only endure certain agonizing moments for a brief period of time, and then one can move along to new and different and more pleasurable times. A new and strange environment will be so for just a little while, and then it becomes familiar. Happily, this is what happened in Greenport.

Greenport provided us with a totally different kind of school experience than any we had ever encountered before this move to Long Island. Greenport High belonged to the New York State Regents system, which means that in order to move from one grade to the next, every student had to pass a series of standardized tests offered by the New York Board of Regents. This in turn meant that the teachers' skills were visibly on the line, and were evaluated on the basis of the number of passes and fails their students received.

The principal of Greenport High School was an iron-jawed man named Joseph Walker, whose main function seemed to be to visit classrooms without advance warning, to see just how well "his teachers" were doing their jobs. He would sit in the back of the room; his jaws set, his face unsmiling, and scowl at teacher and students alike. Mrs. Daly, my English teacher, a perfectly competent, albeit somewhat timid soul, would visibly change the minute "Sneaky Joe" (for so he was dubbed by the irreverent student body) entered the room. She would begin to stammer;

47

her face would grow red, and her voice would tremble. The worst part was watching the beads of perspiration form on her forehead as the fearful Mr. Walker studied her in action.

We tried to pretend that we didn't see these embarrassing changes take place, but we all heaved a great sigh of relief when Iron Jaw—another name for the principal—finally left the room. All these years later, I can still conjure up the sense of tension that entered the room when he did. No wonder he was called Sneaky Joe and Iron Jaw!

One of the nice things about the Regents program was the awards ceremony at the end of the school year. Prizes were given to the students with the highest marks in various fields, and great was the excitement in the school auditorium on Awards Night. Usually the boys won the math prizes, but our first year in Greenport produced a new kind of winner. The auditorium was filled with students and their parents. Mr. Walker stood in the center of the stage and solemnly dispensed the awards. It was when he came to the math award that we felt a certain crackle of excitement in the air, for he started by saying, "We have sometimes had a 97 in Plane Geometry, and a 98 in Advanced Geometry, and a 98 in Intermediate Algebra, but *never* have we had *one hundred* percent in each of these subjects, and all by the *same person*. Will Kate Salter please come up to the stage!" Murmurs of awe and incredulity rippled through the auditorium. This was indeed a brilliant achievement! A particular outburst of joyful applause came from our corner as we watched Kate approach the stage. She looked very little like a mathematics scholar, for she was not only petite, but also very pretty. That was one occasion when we didn't object to having all eyes turned our way.

Another time that stands out in my memory at Greenport High was a day which all who lived through it will never forget. It was the middle of September 1938. The day started like any other school day. Perhaps the only difference was the intense quiet and stillness that imperceptibly pervaded the atmosphere. The air seemed saturated with humidity. Not a leaf on the trees moved; no birds sang. Even the clouds in the sky were motionless. Everywhere there was an enormous quiet.

As I walked to school, I was both conscious and unconscious of a strange feeling in the air. I would not have guessed that, all these years later, I would be able to describe the precise feeling of that day, that very September afternoon.

As the day progressed, the cool of the morning changed gradually into a tempest that developed into one of the greatest hurricanes of the century: the famous Hurricane of 1938. A small wind started up, gradually at first, and then becoming stronger and stronger, until it was as if Poseidon himself had released all the winds of the universe from his mighty bag. And with the wind came rains—dense, torrential, fierce and blinding.

As we sat in the classroom, everyone, from the teacher to the students, found that the swell of sounds and sights from the outside compelled us to forget our current classroom subject matter, and attend to the great natural event which was unfolding all around us. The trees within view not only bent under the force of the great wind, but cracked and broke. We saw them fall. Everyone wanted to leave the school building and get home to be safe and sound. But when we discovered that the front doors of the building wouldn't open because of the powerful pressure of the wind against them, we realized that we were captives in the building. We knew it anyway, of course, because no one would really consider stepping out into such a storm—nor would any school allow any casual student departures.

High noon turned into afternoon; and as the storm pounded on, we students talked and marveled excitedly and fearfully. We also experienced absolute awe. At about three o'clock, there was a slight abatement in the power of the wind. It was still very wet and windy, but the school doors were once more manageable, and this made us eager to be off. To everyone's surprise, telephone lines were still working, so Pat immediately went to the office and called Mother to announce to her that we were "on our way." Mother's shriek of protest was audible almost on the other side of the room, as she demanded "stay absolutely where you are, Patricia!"

A short while later, my grandfather, darling little man that he was (only five feet, eight inches in height to be sure, but all of twelve feet tall in spirit), decided to take matters into his own hands. He set off, on foot, in the wind and the rain, to collect his little family of grandchildren. I will never forget the sight of him in his chocolate brown suit, arriving wet, but smiling, to escort us through the storm-battered streets to the safety of our own home.

The energy and electricity in the air had charged everyone with extra voltage. Because the electricity in town was no longer functioning, all the lights were out, but people were turned on. It was a wild and stimulating atmosphere. Walking home that day was like exploring a strange, exotic land. The quiet, familiar streets where we had walked that very morning were now blocked by fallen trees, broken branches, and bits of wood and paper, all awash in gushing water. Not only that, but it was almost a *tour de force* to walk the distance to our home because of the still-powerful push of the wind. We talked very little; we needed our energy to thread our way through the jumbled streets and against the roaring wind.

The situation at home produced its own anxieties. We found water creeping up past the barn, past the tennis court, lapping gently about seven feet away from the house itself. The inlet, normally quiet and tranquil, was now a raging body of water. As we looked farther out towards Peconic Bay, we could see great whitecaps churned up by the wind as it raced across the water.

What we didn't see then, but saw in abundance during the next few days, were boats, dry-docked, everywhere: on the golf courses, on the roadsides, in backyards, foundering by the docks. The 1938 Hurricane devastated small boats as well as buildings in and around Greenport. The main streets were flooded. The movie theater was washed out. Over 720 trees were uprooted in our town alone. I remember the curious delight of sitting on our front porch after the storm. The regular sidewalk was blocked by the fallen massive oaks that had lined Main Street, so everyone walking along our part of Main Street had to pass close by our porch because of the fallen trees blocking the sidewalk. Never have I experienced more friendliness and good humor than during that week after the hurricane. It is a common bit of knowledge that human beings love to give one another information. In this case we all wanted to tell each other exactly where we had been, and what we had been doing, when the storm struck. Everyone talked, and what is more remarkable, everyone listened.

What an interesting change developed in the pattern of our life as we adjusted to not having electricity. Using candles and kerosene lamps had its own charm. We all went to bed at eight p.m. and found it very pleasant. If we wanted to listen to the radio, we had to go to the car, with its battery-operated radio. This seemed quite dashing to us, and we darted in and out far more often than necessary, just because it was such a novelty. Life was simpler, and yet it was great fun. There is nothing like a change of routine to liven things up!

Tales of the hurricane filled everyone's conversation. I recall the story of the man from

Easthampton, Long Island, who had spent a great deal of money on a barometer purchased at Abercrombie and Fitch. The instrument had arrived on the day of the hurricane, and the new owner was so outraged at the reading, which kept indicating an oncoming hurricane, that he packed it up with a scorching letter of complaint. He set out to mail his letter, but by the time he got home, he found that he had no home. It had been washed out to sea. His was not the only home that was lost in the hurricane. Many of the splendid summer homes in Easthampton and Southampton were destroyed by the massive waves that rolled in during the mighty storm. Ocean roads, buried under tons of sand, were impassable for weeks.

One rather exciting change resulting from the hurricane was local movie-going. Because the storm had knocked out the existing movie theater, a makeshift substitute had been set up in a local church auditorium. This plain, large room held many straight-backed chairs. Although spartan, it had everything we demanded of a movie theater at that time—a screen and a candy counter where one could buy our absolute favorite candy, Jujyfruits, without which no movie was complete. It also had electricity, so that while we waited for the movie to begin, its lights enabled us all to see who was there, and to greet each other, and wait sociably and enthusiastically for the film to begin.

Oh, what a wonderful feeling before the movie started up. The slow build-up: first, the lights off, then the newsreel, and maybe, if we were lucky, a little comedy "short." Following that, immediately prior to the main feature, the previews, revealing next week's movie treats. And then, the great moment— the movie itself!

And what movies there were back in the middle-thirties. We didn't realize that we were in the midst of the golden age of an art form. Douglas Fairbanks, Jr., Charles Boyer, Ronald Coleman, Errol Flynn, Fred Astaire and Ginger Rogers, Irene Dunne, and oh, so many others, created magic on the screen. Movies were awash in costume and music, dancing and singing and joyful emotion.

The Hays Office, which imposed a strict code of conduct on filmmakers, kept the screen fairly free from violence and the graphic depiction of sexual activity, so that one was not a voyeur perforce, in front of the screen, but a willing participant in romance and adventure and wit.

Pat and I would set out from our home, which was about five blocks from the church movie theater, filled with anticipation. We always had enough money for two boxes each of the coveted Jujyfruits—those chewy, gummy candies that heightened the pleasure of every moment of watching that screen. We would sink into our seats and let the magic weave its spell. Afterwards, we would literally dance our way home. There were seldom people on the street, so we had the sidewalk to ourselves. We had invented a two-step routine that took us from one side of the walk to the other. Performing this simple, graceful step, arm in arm, as synchronized as the Rockettes, singing as we went, we would dance our way home. And if we had just seen a musical, we would add the tunes from the show to our exuberant homeward dance, and imitate Eleanor Powell, or Al Jolson, or Fred and Ginger.

We went to the movies at least twice a week. Being great fans, we collected photos of the stars we liked best, and we sometimes found ourselves so overwhelmed by the charms of our favorites that we had to turn their pictures to the wall because we swooned at the sight of them. I remember a long period when all of Charles Boyer's photographs, so carefully cut out of movie magazines and so lovingly affixed to our bedroom walls, had to be turned face-in. He was just too appealing! If anyone really wanted to undo us, they had only to imitate Boyer's rich French accent. Only Douglas Fairbanks, Jr. offered him any competition.

One little extra movie treat was the result of Pat's hair-do. She wore her hair like Deanna Durbin, who was at the height of her popularity in the late '30s, and was about the same age as Pat. Also, Pat looked a little like Deanna. Normally, this would not have occasioned much interest, but in Greenport, on a Sunday afternoon, when all the kids in town were together in the makeshift theater, it was an event when the "new girl" walked in. They took to calling out "Hi, Deanna!" when they spied Pat, and it got so they almost believed that she was, if not actually Deanna Durbin, then perhaps someone famous in her own right. For my part, I loved the reflected glory that came with sister Pat's fame as a Deanna Durbin look-alike.

In those days, the movies created the illusion that if you follow the rules, everything works out. It may be that we knew this wasn't actually the way things are, but it was grand to imagine that it might be so. It created a rosy feeling of optimism in people. We all felt good after going to the movies. It was fun to see a world flooded with sunlight where good triumphs over evil. I am not sure that we gain by perceiving the world in drabs and blacks.

But it was not only the doors of the movie theater and of school that opened for us in Greenport. There were other doors which seemed like golden gates to new feelings and new sights, and which brought us into touch with people and adventures we had never before experienced.

We had always been more or less the black sheep in my mother's family. Her brothers and only sister were all conservative and conventional. They didn't know what to make of Mother's unorthodox approach to life, and they also did not much care for the fact that Granddad so willingly helped our family out financially. Mother, who was so truly unconventional that she didn't realize that she was, felt deeply pained by the coolness of her brothers and sister. We children were quite oblivious to it, and didn't even know that we were not part of the inner circle. To use the parlance of the day, we could have cared less. All of this changed, however, in Greenport, because we had Granddad living with us. Plus, now we had a spacious, wonderful house and were living practically on the shores of Peconic Bay.

All of our lives, we had heard Mother speak of the wonderful times she and her cousins had had when she was growing up. She told us about houseboat trips on the Mississippi River, family reunions, clam digs in Cutchogue, and songfests in the twilight on the spacious lawn of Aunt Lily and Uncle George's elegant home. Her recollections sounded grand to us—grand, and completely out of reach. But now we discovered what she was talking about! Handsome young cousins came by to visit Granddad, and stayed on after they discovered that not only was Granddad in this wonderful house on the edge of the sea, but so were three pretty and lively cousins. Our mutual delight was boundless. Discovering a cousin of one's own age is almost like finding a new brother or sister. We couldn't believe the fun it was to suddenly have these wonderful cousins staying in the house where we could sing, play games, swim, laugh, or, as the saying goes, just "hang out" together.

Pat and our cousin Jack, the oldest son of Mother's brother Harry, formed a close attachment to each other. I, who was so close to Pat, shared all the excitement of their innocent romance without having to endure any of its stress. I remember sitting in the front seat of the car with them, and being aware that their little fingers were touching, and of feeling the same surge of excitement that they felt. It was a lovely, uncomplicated and innocent romance, and they seemed to enjoy my passive participation in it almost as much as I did. Little did we dream then that dear Jack would die in World War II—shot down as he piloted his fighter plane over Alexandria, Egypt—lost forever in those distant sands. And thank heavens we did not know it, for had we known, we could never have had those golden days we treasured so much.

The door through which our cousins walked was a wonderful one, and it made yet another newly opened door even more delightful for all of us. I refer to the unalloyed joy we felt when we discovered what it was like to have a car in the family. We had never owned a car. Granddad had always owned one, and now that we all lived together in Greenport, we reaped the benefits of motorized transportation. Granddad's car was a perfectly plain grey Ford—serviceable, functional, but not at all striking.

I still clearly remember one summer afternoon when I was sitting idly on the front porch of 726 Main Street in Greenport. Suddenly, a sleek, elegant, forest-green sedan turned into the driveway. The tires of this vehicle were white walled, and the design was smashingly new. Never had I seen such a shape on a car as this one had! Instantly, my idleness vanished, and I looked with keen interest to see not only the car, but the driver as well. Talk about a double take, the driver was none other than Granddad. There he sat in the driver's seat, pink-cheeked, smiling, and eyes sparkling with fun. By now, I had let out such a whoop of delight that it brought the others running to the front porch. Oh, how we all shouted and shrieked and laughed and queried and marveled at this wonderful new car.

Granddad loved a surprise, and this was his surprise for all of us: a Mercury, Ford's newest creation, a first, and ours! The white walled tires, which I had never seen before in my life, provided the final touch to this stunning new machine. It was, to describe it in the language of the day, *smooth*, and it belonged in our driveway. There may be—there surely are—cars more elegant, more beautiful, more costly and more magnificent, but for me there will never be another car like that Mercury. You have to have never owned a car to fully appreciate the new dimensions of the world that opens up when a car comes into your life—and particularly a car that is a "first-timer," for this was the first year the Mercury had been manufactured.

Granddad's new car opened up doors for us which led to all of Greenport, to Long Island Sound, to salt sea marshes, to coves and bays, and above all, to the ocean. My, it was fun.

Town Beach, Greenport's only local swimming spot, was four miles from town. The sandy beach was wide and clean, and the water was the way water used to be—clear and flowing, and free from any kind of pollution. Right in the middle of the beach area was a wonderful little hamburger joint called "Jack's Shack." I am sure that Jack has long been dead, but his specialty, the perfect hamburger, will live forever in my memory. He used lean red meat, molded into a thick patty, grilled to perfect doneness, and topped with onions, pickles, ketchup, and a dab of mustard, packed into a large, solid warm bun. This perfect hamburger was all ours for only five cents. Oh, the heaven of eating one of Jack's specialty burgers, after a great swim in the Sound is one of those long-loved activities that will never come again.

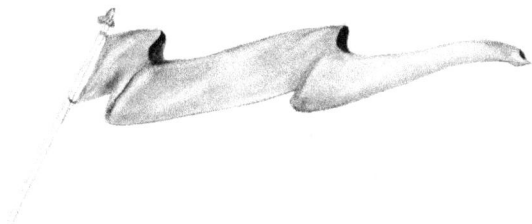

CHAPTER FOUR

Not only did 1938 bring the great hurricane, but the year was very significant in our lives for other reasons, though we didn't know to what degree until much later. It was a year that brought us something very dear and new and exciting, and it was also a year that initiated the gradual loss of someone very important to us.

We, along with all of Greenport, found ourselves agog with excitement at the news that "Mrs. Salter was pregnant!" Although we of course knew that our father had paid a family Christmas visit at the end of 1937, many people in town were unaware of this fact. When the gracious and lovely Mrs. Salter began to show signs of her pregnancy, there was understandable puzzlement at this new development. One of the charming things about life in a small town is the shared concern of everybody in everybody's business. Mrs. Townsend, engagingly called "Diamond Lil" by the townspeople because of her eminent position as owner and manager of the town's biggest business, The Townsend Manor Inn, was Mother's great champion. It was she who had sponsored Mother for membership in the town's literary club, The Shakespeare Club, and it was she who countered the small-town gossip about Mother's forthcoming baby with the stern reminder to everyone that Professor Salter had come for a Christmas visit. Mother was no more aware of the hubbub about her pregnancy than she had been about the great honor conferred on her by the invitation to join the exclusive Shakespeare Club. She took both events as they came. She was happy about this pregnancy, albeit a little concerned because she was now in her forties and this was admittedly risky. None of us apparently had ever been planned for, so the coming of the new baby was as unexpected as the others had been, and was equally welcome to Mother.

As for us, we were ecstatic. The thought of having our own baby filled us with the greatest joy. Each of us saw ourselves as a favorite older sibling, and we rejoiced in the coming event. The hospital where the baby was to be born was located right across the creek from our house. We could see it from the kitchen window. Spacious and homelike, surrounded by a grove of flourishing poplar trees, it seemed almost like an extension of 726 Main Street. The only problem for us was that it would take months to bring this great occurrence to pass. That seemed like a long, long time to wait.

And it did indeed seem a long time to poor Mother. She was stricken with every negative symptom of pregnancy that one could have. Her bedroom was right next to the kitchen where our wonderful cook, a great fat lady named Julie, worked her culinary magic. This was splendid for us because it meant three good meals a day (Granddad's beneficence at work again), but it meant trouble for Mother because the same odors that so tantalized us—bacon and coffee and onions and garlic—were the very ones that made Mother ill. Morning sickness came on with vigor, and stayed.

Because of her age, the doctor wanted her on the first floor, so that she would not have to go up and down stairs, and he wanted her "lying low." Being the kind of woman she was, she needed to occupy her mind, so rather than merely lying idly in bed, she turned her attention to newspapers—to the *New York Times* and the *Christian Science Monitor*. These years were deeply troubled, and the papers were full of the news of the day. As we know now, of course, in 1938 the world was on the brink of World War II, and there were violent differences of opinion on the subject of intervention versus isolationism. It was a time of seething passions. People responded intensely to the burning issues of the day.

Mother had plenty of time to read and think about the state of the world. The monstrous activity of the Germans and Italians filled her with horror, and she came down vigorously on the side of the interventionists. Since there were many advocates presenting the isolationist point of view, she felt strongly provoked to present the other side, and to that end began writing letters to the editor of the *New York Times*. Her letters were forceful and vivid. They offered incisive reasons for intervention, and they elicited immediate response from representatives of both points of view. Suddenly, Mother had become quite a voice for those who saw Germany as a world threat.

At the same time the world was in the throes of the agitation and disruption created by Nazi Germany, another problem thrust itself upon the consciousness of the civilized world. What could the country do with all the people who had fled Germany for their lives, and wanted now to come to the United States? Mother thought about this problem, talked about it, wrote about it. One night, in the middle of the night, she had an inspiration that amounted almost to a vision.

She visualized the United States welcoming and sponsoring individual refugee families—not just in the big cities, but also in small towns throughout the country. She called her plan "A Family to a City," and it was her idea that each sponsoring community would form a committee whose task it would be to raise enough money to bring one family into its midst. The committee would provide a job, housing, and sufficient financial backing for the family so that it could survive until it was able to provide for itself. A minimum-maximum of one year was suggested, at the end of which time the new family would presumably be standing strongly on its own feet. The beauty of the plan was, of course, that no one town would be burdened with so many refugees that it would be impossible to absorb them all. Instead, there would be many towns that could absorb the many people who clamored to come to the United States, and who needed refuge.

Mother gathered together a group of people who responded favorably to her idea, and soon had organized a committee to try it out. Albert Einstein, who summered in nearby Cutchogue, was one of the committee members. He had agreed to speak on behalf of the scheme to the assembly of townsfolk who met to learn more about it. It was indeed exciting when, on the night of the big town meeting in Southold, he took his seat next to Mother at the long table in the front of the room. When he rose to talk to us about the plan, we all stared in awe and disbelief. Einstein himself, in the same room with us. Pat shook his hand (as we all did), and claimed that she would never wash her right hand again. The most wonderful fact, though, was that he supported Mother's plan.

In time, the committee brought to town a very talented German film editor and her two small children. Eva W. had been the wife of a successful filmmaker in Berlin. She and her husband had worked together in the German film industry until Hitler came into power. The family then broke up, because Eva was Jewish. Her husband's fear of the consequences of being wed to a Jew was greater than his love for her, so they separated. Eva and her two little girls, Lisa and Anna Marie, somehow got themselves to New York City. Unable to find any way to support her little family, Eva almost miraculously found out about the Greenport Refugee Committee, and was soon in our town where she would spend the summer, and would be given enough time and support to organize her new life. I can clearly recall the profound gratitude of this besieged woman. She was tired when she arrived—bone-tired, from the emotional and physical stress of immigrating, and separating, and not knowing what was to become of her. Finding a niche, albeit a temporary one, in a lovely town at the edge of the shining waters of Peconic Bay, with people who welcomed her and made her know they cared about her, was overwhelming. Her gratitude seemed limitless. The children were six and four when we met them, unable to utter a word of English. But they learned quickly, and we made friends easily.

Mother was thrilled by the results of her plan, and it was a happy time for all of us. Little did I know then what a profound effect her refugee work would have on our lives. But that's part of the fun of life—the unexpectedness of it all!

The "unexpected" baby arrived on schedule—our beautiful brother Christopher Lord, promptly dubbed "Kit." How quickly did we grow accustomed to his merry presence. His was a lovely disposition, and somehow he was always being held by a sister or brother, or Mother, or a friend who might be in the house. I remember the arrival of a stranger who was introducing himself as a friend of a friend, when one of us came through the room holding Kit, and asked him to "hold the baby for a minute." I think the bewildered stranger was still holding Kit twenty minutes later and no doubt wondering what kind of a zany household he had wandered into.

Mother's political activities did not cease when Kit was born. On the contrary, she became ever more absorbed in the doings of the world. There always seemed to be one more letter to write, one more article to answer, and one more meeting to attend. The change in Mother came on slowly, but it did come ever so surely, so that we, without knowing it, were losing this dear and precious woman as we had known her. Her true focus of attention was now on the world and its enormous problems; and as a result, there was very little room in her attention or feelings for us, which is why I began this part of my story by saying that 1938 brought us one treasure, and took another treasure away from us. How dearly we loved the one, and how we grieved at the loss of the other. Mother's really intense political involvement, however, was still mostly in the future; back in 1938 and 1939 there were many pleasant excursions, both on land and water, which occupied us, chief of which perhaps was our indefatigable pursuit of our love of saltwater.

When one travels through Suffolk County in Long Island today, it is hard to imagine the roads as we found them back in '37 and '38. At that time, they were almost devoid of traffic. Often, it was just us in Granddad's car, on a deserted road that skirted the Atlantic Ocean. What a temptation this placed before us—the temptation to go fast, really fast! I wish I could say that we resisted that temptation, but I can't. We didn't. We had stretches on those wonderful roads where we tore along at ninety miles an hour. Cousin Jack was a great driver, and we were admiring and willing passengers. In retrospect, I am shocked at what we did, but while we were in the midst of it—while we were actually doing it—it seemed exciting and fun and danger-free. So much for the judgment of youth.

Southampton and Easthampton's beaches were our favorite ocean targets, but before we got there, we always drove through town. Those towns, the Hamptons, were then, as they are now, the mecca for the rich and the tanned, those we called at that time "the station wagon crowd." In those days, station wagons were only owned by the rich. Usually a name on the door in small print identified what estate the car was from. Names like *High Hill* or *Dune Breakers* or *Salt Spray* were fashionable. Kate, Pat and I felt that the highest compliment we could give, was to say that someone looked "station wagon," and if anyone ever told us that we looked station wagon, we simply beamed with self satisfaction and were quite obnoxious for as long as it took the compliment to wear off.

The Hamptons were filled with small shops, which were quite different from any shops we had seen. We call them boutiques today and they were great fun to look in on through the window. If, however, we were ever bold enough to enter, we quickly realized our mistake. The shops were staffed by women who seemed to derive their fun by acting as snooty as they could. They could not exercise this manner upon the people they were imitating, but they surely knew how to intimidate the likes of us. It didn't take them long to make us feel hopelessly gauche and from the wrong side of the tracks. We always got out very fast.

But the true satisfaction of those days came when we had left the towns behind and reached the beach, the long sandy stretches of shoreline where we would find our private spot, spread out our blankets and then ourselves, and settle in for the real business of the day—which was to get a tan of our own. And what tans we got. It was as if, by the end of the day, the sun, the sand, the saltwater, and the surf had melded, and become part of us. I looked more like a lobster than a human being, at the end of one of these days; but ultimately it was worth it, because the bright red color turned to golden brown, and I did indeed look almost station wagon!

On some days we would take the makings for an evening picnic. Watching the moon come up over the sea, hearing the punch of the waves against the shore, feeling a little sticky from the saltwater in which we had swum all day, produced a perfect blend of feeling, sight and sound. We usually sang around the campfire before heading home, leaving the mighty ocean and returning happily to our own salt marsh inlet.

Although it is lovely to live where there is a salt marsh inlet in your own backyard, what is even lovelier came into our lives during our first year in Greenport. It was totally unexpected, and it happened—as did so many of the joys in our life—because of Granddad.

One day in spring, on a regular school day, Granddad announced that he wanted us all to be at home in the early afternoon. He wouldn't tell us why, saying only that he and his nephew, Mother's 250-pound cousin Linn, who lived in nearby Cutchogue, needed us. I, who ordinarily never minded missing a day of school, was quite upset at this demand of Granddad's, because on that particular day I did not want to stay home from school. Such is the perverse nature of youth.

In any case, our scheduled appointment with Granddad was for one-thirty. One-thirty came and went; two-thirty came and went. By half-past three, I was ready to scream. Waiting is not my long suit, and having to wait at home when I wanted to be in school compounded my restlessness and ill-temper. How well I recall my misery as I marked the time, doing nothing, just waiting. And then suddenly Granddad appeared. We typically heard the sound of the Mercury pulling up to the house, but this time he had come through the back door and was chuckling.

"Hello, girls," he said. "Come with me."

"Where have you *been*, Granddad?" I almost wailed.

"Come and see," he replied. We immediately did just that.

We followed him through the house, out the back door, and down through the yard to our little pier, which jutted out into the inlet. There sat Cousin Linn, tranquil and gigantic, in a large, out-sized rowboat equipped with an outboard motor.

"Get in, girls!" said Granddad.

"*Get in?*" we shrieked. "Whose boat is this? What's happening?"

"This is our boat," said Granddad. "Our boat, your boat, the family boat. A body can't live on the water without a boat, now can they? And we live on the water, don't we? So now we have a boat. And since we do, what do you say to our giving Cousin Linn a ride home?"

Well, such joy and delight and celebration can scarcely be imagined!

We all climbed aboard and, with Linn at the helm, we slowly moved down the creek, out into Peconic Bay, staying close to the shoreline, and reached Linn's point of destination in short order.

All regrets about having missed school were gone, and all our restlessness and ill temper vanished into the ether. We could think of nothing except of the boat—that it was ours, absolutely ours, and that it would soon be anchored securely at our own dock.

Now the smell of the saltwater was as near to us as the surface on which we putted about, and my, how we did putt! Our new favorite summer activity became anything that had to do with the *On Wisconsin*, for so we named our grand new boat. We took long day trips, or sometimes even an overnight camping trip.

These voyages, of course, could only be undertaken with an adult in tow, as it were. It is here that our father, who until now had been a fairly dim figure in our lives, came in and became more important. Dockie, like Mother, was a great audience. He spearheaded many activities; such as reading Shakespeare's plays aloud, memorizing and declaiming passages from prose and poetry, discussing the writings of Edmund Burke and other political writers. I recall even that we were not given permission to go to a movie unless we wrote a review of the film after we had seen it. We wrote our critiques in the discarded "blue books" which were in use at the university for student examinations. Dockie made us aware of the role of ideas in the world, and he made us very conscious of writing style. In fact, writing a letter, to him, was a tense experience, because one knew that one was always expected to be interesting which was a daunting challenge for the best of us.

For years, this rigid criterion did much to slow me down as a correspondent. The *demand* to be witty and fascinating dried up my ability to be either.

Nonetheless, we loved spending time with Dockie. To our delight, he took a vacation from his customary teaching in summer school, and spent the summer of 1939 with us. It was then that our greatest fun began, when we took camping trips in the *On Wisconsin*. We would load the boat up with mattresses (we were pampered "campers"!), a small Coleman stove, food and books, fishing tackle for Dockie, and off we would go! Greenport, remember, is situated on Peconic Bay, which in turn opened onto Gardiner's Bay, and Gardiner's Bay eventually flowed into the ocean, so there seemed unlimited miles of water and coastline to explore.

One particular trip was to be our last, for we were scheduled to move back to Wisconsin at the end of the week. We wanted this trip to be the biggest and best of them all. We jokingly told neighbors that we might go as far as Gardiner's Island, a place I had once visited as part of a tour, and knew it to be not only very beautiful, but also very privately owned, and closed to trespassers. Native Greenporters laughed at our casual reference to Gardiner's Island, and claimed that, in the first place, our "old boat" wouldn't begin to get that far; and that if, by some chance, it did reach those forbidden shores, we would be shot on sight as trespassers.

Our talk was, of course, just idle chatter. We had, in fact, no way of knowing exactly where we would land. We knew only that this August 19th, 1939 was a shimmering summer day, and ideal for our final camping venture. We loaded the *On Wisconsin* with lots of books, food and equipment, pulled the trusty outboard motor cord, and chugged out towards the blue waters of Peconic Bay.

The day was so fine that we almost forgot there was an objective other than simply being on the water. We putted along, often in the company of friendly porpoises who swam along at our side. The day seemed timeless as we glided across the water, immersed in sun and air, breathing in the fragrance of the saltwater beneath us. Eventually, however, one of us observed that the sun was beginning to sink a bit, and that since we were quite far out from shore, we needed to seek shelter. No time to find the "perfect" campsite; we needed to head for the nearest land to avoid being caught on the water at night.

We set our boat at once on course for the closest shore we could see. Even at the zipping speed of four knots an hour, it took well over an hour to reach it; and to our dismay, we saw immediately that the beach proved to be no beach at all, but a slender strip of land at the foot of a high cliff. Because the tide was low, it was visible now; but at high tide it would be completely covered by water.

We were horrified by this discovery, but when we spied a small promontory, high and dry, jutting out from the cliff, we felt partial relief. We at least could be snug for the night, though our boat would have to weather the choppy waters—a state of affairs that disturbed us because the waves were breaking with considerable force upon the shore.

We had no alternative, however, so we unloaded the necessary goods and carried them up to the safe haven of the promontory. It was a secure and cozy spot for us, and we were both happy and efficient as we settled down for the night. Unfortunately, the loud noise of the waves pounding against the shore kept us from falling asleep, and we anxiously looked down to see how our boat was faring. To our horror, we saw that it had filled with water! The waves were breaking over the boat rather than under it. Since we had already lifted the outboard motor out of the boat and stashed it, and since there was in any case no place where we could pull the boat itself, there was nothing we could do to improve the situation. We would simply have to wait for low tide the next day, when we would bail out the boat and make it once more ready for travel.

The next morning, I was the first one awake. I lay on my back and gazed at the morning sky while watching the osprey fly overhead and feeling that this was indeed the best of all camping trips. I stretched and sat up, and decided to have a look at the boat. Imagine my feelings when I looked down and saw that there was *no* boat! The *On Wisconsin* had vanished completely. Correction please, not quite completely. Looking out across the water, a little beyond the shoreline, I saw a white board drifting by; and by now, with Pat and Dockie awake, we spotted more pieces of wreckage down the beach. The "old debbil sea" had demolished our trusty, beloved *On Wisconsin*.

Pat and I were thrilled at this turn of events. This was adventure with a capital A! We, at fourteen and fifteen, were very romantic, and to suddenly find ourselves shipwrecked on some strange Long Island shore seemed too grand for words. My father, who was somewhat more practical (although, it must be confessed, not a great deal more so), was more aware of our position; we were stuck somewhere in the middle of nowhere with two single mattresses, an outboard motor, a gasoline stove, and other odds and ends. All in all, he was not as delighted as we were. However, even he succumbed to the magic of the perfect summer day, and after a simple breakfast, his good spirits matched ours as we set forth in search of help. Pat and I were both wearing shorts, and were barefoot, having unwittingly left our shoes in the boat. Ah well! This would only add spice to our story—shipwrecked, and barefoot to boot! What a wonderful combination of disasters!

Because the tide was at ebb, we were able to walk along the narrow strip of shore, and this we did for what seemed a very long time. Finally, since we found nothing in front of us but endless sand and water, we decided that we must climb the cliff and strike into the center of land where we would surely find someone with a phone. We would then call home and make arrangements for our rescue.

We would figure some way to get our possessions from the beach.

With this loosely formulated plan in mind, we scrambled up the cliff, expecting at the very least to see a road or something suggesting civilization. How wrong we were. What we found, as far as the eye could see, was land, densely covered with thick, compact green bushes, small wind-gnarled trees, briar patches and thickets, where not even a faint path was visible. We were in a completely wild countryside. Pheasants darted out in front of us as we walked; deer started up in the brush ahead of us; and overhead, the ubiquitous osprey swooped and rose in the cloudless sky.

Poor Pat and I found the going pretty rough. We were covered with scratches from head to toe. Yet, in spite of this discomfort, and the bewilderment we were beginning to experience at being lost in this unexpected wilderness, we were enchanted by the beauty of land, sky, and the soaring birds. The place was full of every kind of life—except human.

We had walked perhaps three miles when, all of

a sudden, I saw a cow, and I can remember making a fantastically profound statement: "Where there are cows, there are men." Actually, it was only the remains of men we came across first, for a little beyond the spot where the cow stood, we came upon a small, enclosed cemetery. We paused, went in through the ancient, creaking gate, and read the gravestones, one by one: Lion Gardiner, Third Lord of the Manor; John Gardiner, Second Lord of the Manor; and so on, down the line. As I mentioned above, I had once been on a tour to the fabled Gardiner's Island, and had seen these stones at that time. I knew now where we were, and I solemnly and with deep excitement announced to Dockie and Pat: "We are on Gardiner's Island!"

This revelation gave us pause, for we knew how private this property was, and we had heard reports from the natives in Greenport of what happened to trespassers on this private and secluded land. We had been told, "People are shot on sight." Nevertheless, there was nothing to do but proceed, and this we did, though with quite a bit of trepidation.

We came first to a group of small houses, rather run-down in appearance, and flanking what appeared to be a great white manor house. We approached the Manor House from the rear. There was no getting out of it now; we must go forward and announce ourselves—uninvited guests. We knocked on the back door, and shortly were confronted with a plain fellow in work clothes who emerged from the kitchen, and looked at us without much expression. Dockie, who was of course our spokesman, stepped forward and explained our situation. The man then gazed at us in complete wonderment. "You'll have to see the boss," he said. "I'll tell him." He directed us towards the front of the house.

The house was set on a hill overlooking a vast body of deep blue water. In the front hallway, we were greeted in a courteous, yet somewhat distant, fashion by a good-looking, sun-tanned man in his middle fifties, who introduced himself as Baron Bror Von Blixen. We learned later that he was the Blix of Isak Dinesen fame in *Out of Africa*. My father again told his story, of how we had camped unknowingly on the Island, and how the waves had washed our boat away during the night. The Baron, much as the workman had done, gazed at us in astonishment, but said very little. We all stood there saying nothing, until suddenly, down the long hallway, like a fresh gust of cool wind, came a tall, wonderfully handsome man of about thirty, who made our current hero, Errol Flynn, look like a weakling. In a beautiful English accent he shouted, "They tell me two beautiful girls have been shipwrecked on my island, but damn it, I don't believe it! Won't you come in? Guest is my name—Winston Guest, and I am delighted to meet you."

Pat and I, overwhelmed by his charm, his enthusiasm, and his courtesy, were conquered on the spot. We fell in love with him then and there, and it was a long, long time before we were interested in any other male—child, boy, or man. And we were totally ignorant of his world class skill as a Polo player!

Mr. Guest seemed to feel about our adventure as we did; something like this didn't happen every day, and we knew that we needed to make the most of it. He led us down the long, walnut-paneled hallway into a large, comfortable living room where, when seated, we again told our story. He insisted that we go upstairs to refresh ourselves. Shortly, there appeared a formally attired maid who ushered us up to one of the front bedrooms, whose windows opened wide onto the sweeping lawns that led to the water's edge. The maid provided us with an elaborate array of cosmetics and toiletries, most of which we had no idea what to do with, but which nevertheless filled us with excitement and delight. There was a small panel on the wall of the bathroom with buttons labeled Butler, Maid, Kitchen, etc., and Pat and I thought this was just about the peak of elegance. Home was never like this in our world.

When we came downstairs once again, Winston Guest insisted that we spend the day and see the entire Island. He had already dispatched some of his workers to retrieve our camping gear, and was now prepared to devote himself to our entertainment. First of all, though, we had to call Mother. I can still remember her response to our opening statement, that we had been shipwrecked on Gardiner's Island, and would be spending the day with Winston Guest. Mother laughed outright and said, "For heaven's sake, you people. Where are you really? Stop this silly game." It was only after Winston took over the phone call in a most masterful way, and told his version of the tale, that she believed us. She knew that the voice she heard was the real thing. Not even a member of the Star Players could produce so perfect a performance as this. What a magical day!

After a sumptuous lunch of lobster, chicken, ham, pheasant, fresh fruit, cheeses, and French-baked bread dripping with butter, we climbed into a very old station wagon, battered even to the point of having no door on the driver's side. Winston leapt into this vehicle with one bound, and we followed as swiftly as possible, and away we went—for the grand tour. Some of the time, we drove over faintly marked roads that were barely discernible; but for the most part, we simply struck out over open fields. As we drove, Winston pointed out to us the things he wanted us to see: the Wishing Well, where you dropped your pennies to make your wishes come true; the spot where Captain Kidd, another uninvited guest, had buried his treasure; the old windmill, in front of the Manor House, where the first Gardiners had ground their wheat; the several lovely freshwater ponds scattered over the hills which looked out over the bay.

We went to a beautiful spot called Whale Hill where we had a go at clay pigeon shooting. This was my first contact with a rifle, and I was afraid I almost wore out my welcome by resting against the rifle with the muzzle in the ground while I awaited my turn. Not even this gaffe, however, dulled our host's graciousness. We didn't know then that Winston, a cousin of Sir Winston Churchill, was a multi-millionaire who belonged to the first families of both the United States and England. We knew only that we had never met such a person before.

Even perfect days have to end. When the time came to walk down to the boat that would carry us across the three miles of water to the mainland, we said our farewells with a heavy heart. To say goodbye to such a man as Winston Guest, after the miracle of simply meeting such a man, was indeed difficult to do. As we said goodbye, we thought we were doing so forever. But once again, Winston dazzled and surpassed all expectations. Not only did we return to the Island, but we did so many times. Winston never tired of presenting Pat and me to his friends and houseguests as "my beautiful shipwrecks"; and Dockie, cast in the role of absent-minded professor, was a popular figure in the Island crowd—a real character.

During our many visits to the Island, we came to know many people—all of them rich, and some of them very rich. Some I liked, and some I didn't. None of them seemed as gracious and wonderful as Winston, who was in a class all by himself. But because we came to the Island so often, we did become a part of the group, and I learned a lesson close-up that has stood me in good stead all of my life. I saw how little "money makes the man." I saw that whether you have a million dollars or a hundred dollars, your worries and concerns are pretty much the same; only the scale is different. Getting an intimate look at the cream of international society prepared me for any society thereafter. It is as if I could not be fooled because I had seen the top and realized that the people who lived "up there" were only human, like the rest of us. What made one stand out was not what was in the pocketbook, but what was in the heart and head. This insight has been consistently useful to me.

But what is the history of this magic island? Fortunately, I had learned some of it when I was here on the earlier tour. The history I remembered went back to the year 1639 when Long Island teemed with Indians. Into this world came a bold and self-confident engineer, Lion Gardiner, with his wife Mary and his small son David. They came from England via Holland to Connecticut, where Lion was involved in building Fort Saybrook at the mouth of the Connecticut River. While he was there, a period of three years, their son was born. This birth was recorded as being the first birth of a white person in the state of Connecticut.

When the work at Fort Saybrook was completed, Lion decided to strike out on his own. It was then that he made his first trip to Long Island. Unfortunately, there are few details about this journey. We do know, however, that when he arrived in Long Island, near what is now Easthampton, he successfully did two things: made friends with Chief Wyandanch, who was the chief of the Montaukett Indians on Long Island, and purchased from Chief Wyandanch the piece of land which we know today as Gardiner's Island. The Gardiners knew it as the Isle of Wight. To the Indians, it was Manchonake. According to some lore, the purchase price for the island was ten bolts of cloth; or, according to another source, a big black dog, a rifle, and a few pieces of cloth!

What did Lion Gardiner receive for this sum? Thirty-three hundred acres of land, seven miles at its longest, and three miles at its widest. This was not mere bare, rocky land. It had rich soil, many fresh water ponds, woods and hills. It was a truly diverse and rich plot of ground. Located three miles from Long Island and ten miles from Easthampton, it is utterly remote, yet accessible by water and, as Winston later demonstrated, accessible also by air.

Gardiner was given sovereignty over everything and everyone on the Island. A deed, first from the Indians, and then from the king, made Gardiner the Lord of the Manor. This right he must have exercised, for I remember seeing in one of the oldest houses on the grounds a chessboard carved into the floor. I was told that this game board had been made by prisoners locked in this room by command of the 'Lord of the Manor.'

Lion Gardiner had purchased the island with farming in mind, and he farmed zealously. Many of the Indians who were living on the land when he bought it stayed on and worked for him so that his work—and crops—prospered. The friendship between Gardiner and Wyandanch is the kind of relationship between Indian and White man that one has often seen depicted in movies, but has never been sure existed in real life. Theirs was a warm and enduring relationship.

At one time Wyandanch was required by some English officials to answer charges of a murder he was alleged to have committed. Wyandanch was not guilty, and wanted to represent himself in his own defense. The members of his tribe were so wary of the English that they urged their chief not to go. It was only when Gardiner stepped forward and offered himself as hostage until Wyandanch returned, that the tribe was satisfied. Toward the end of his life, Wyandanch gave Gardiner the entire piece of land on which Smithtown, Long Island lies. This he did merely as a token of his gratitude. In addition, he made Gardiner the guardian of his son, who would succeed him as chief.

After Gardiner's death in 1653, his wife Mary became the sole owner of the island. She entailed it to the male heirs of Lion and Mary. The remarkable thing about this place is that, even though it was settled so long ago by the first white settlers in New York State, the island is still owned by the Gardiner family.[1]

Every island has its own romantic story, and Gardiner's Island is no exception. Captain Kidd, the most famous pirate of them all, came a-calling, and left some of his treasure there—or so the story goes. There are two accounts of his alleged visit: one is that he came in, took what he needed, and then showed John Gardiner where he had buried the treasure, saying to him, "You may have this if I don't come back; but if I come back and find it gone, I will have your head, or the head of one of your sons!" The other, and less ferocious, version states that Captain Kidd came, dropped anchor in Gardiner's Bay, paid for everything he took, and asked permission to bury some goods, not specifying what they were, but promising that he would be back for them. It wasn't until much later, when officials who were investigating the activities of the famous pirate called him to Boston, that Gardiner learned it was Captain Kidd with whom he had been dealing. The Boston commissioners unearthed and confiscated the treasure, which consisted of gold bars, gold dust, silver, and precious, unpolished stones. A handsome stone marking the spot where the treasure was buried now commemorates this tale.

Although the Island is still in the hands of the Gardiner family, and is still very much as it was when it was settled some three hundred years ago, it has not always been occupied by Gardiners. In earlier days, it was rented out as farmland; and, more recently, it has been leased as a game preserve. The Island abounds with wild game, and has thus become a wonderful hunting ground for sportsmen. But, whether it be a hunter's paradise or a farm, when one stands by the old windmill, high on a hill looking out over the deep blue waters of Gardiner's Bay, one senses the life that has gone on in this enchanting spot. And very little has changed since it was bought in exchange for ten bolts of cloth. Three hundred years slipped away. That doesn't happen very often.

Pat and I were quite insufferable after this great adventure. We swooned over Winston, and did little else but talk about him, and the Island, and the Baron, and the Rockefellers, and any other guest whose name we thought of. We looked with scorn on boys our own age. What could a youth of fifteen or sixteen possibly have to interest us, who had been spending time with a giant like Winston Guest?

At first, all of our friends were as entranced as

we were by our adventure, and they listened to our accounts with rapt attention and a certain amount of envy. But in time, they grew weary of the subject. They had had enough, and were ready to throw us off of a rooftop. How splendid that time has a way of calming even the most intense emotions because, in time, we did come back to ourselves, which made life easier for everyone.

[1] [Editor's Note: Much has been written of the dramatic and romantic story of Gardiner's Island, which has become quite fashionable in that area. If any reader wishes to get further detail and additional references, one source is *Origins of the Past: The Story of Montauk and Gardiner's Island*. (The East Hampton Historical Collection.) Ed. Tom Twomey. 2013.]

CHAPTER FIVE

Returning to Madison after the two years in
Greenport helped a great deal in the process of
getting back to the way we were "before Winston."
Actually, we greeted the plan to return with delight.
It meant not only going back to a school we had
loved, but also going back to many good friends.

This time, we were particularly thrilled about
going home because we actually had a house to go
to—a home of our own. Granddad had bought a
house on a comfortable residential street on the west
side of town, near Madison's great Vilas Park and
Zoo, and within easy walking distance of Wisconsin
High School. The address was: 1610 Adams Street.
What a world those numbers conjure up—1610! It is
as if all the other houses in Madison fall away when

Jean Salter Roetter

I say those numbers. We quickly began to speak of the new house merely as 1610, and when any of us talks about it today, a half-century or more later, we still refer to it as 1610.

It wasn't a beautiful house—quite the contrary. A more box-like, unimaginative dwelling could scarcely be imagined. It was, however, ours—entirely ours; there was no landlord to scold us or admonish us; there was no one above us nor beneath us. It was just our family ensconced in its own private quarters!

There were eight rooms—which meant that all had their own room, except for Pat and me, and we were glad to share a room once again. We never ran out of things to talk about, and what better time to talk than at night before falling asleep. Granddad had a splendid basement in which he could put up his taffy hooks and make his famous molasses taffy. Dockie had a little extra cubbyhole of a room on the third floor, which he turned into a darkroom where he could develop the many pictures he took with his impractically expensive camera. Joel had a room on that same floor, where he was able to pursue his efforts to develop a Charles Atlas body. Mother had a piano in the living room where she could play her Chopin etudes and the slow parts of her favorite Beethoven sonatas. Kate managed to develop a most feminine atmosphere in her bedroom, where she had all the privacy she demanded, and where she could pine over her current boyfriend. And Kit, the merry, ebullient, happy little love of our life, had a neat little nursery at the top of the stairs.

Walking into 1610 was like walking into a club; everyone was busy doing something. Dockie, who loved oatmeal, might be in the kitchen boiling up a pot of it. If he were, there was nothing he liked better than to have one of us join him for a chat. When he invited you to join him, you felt as if an honor had been conferred on you, and you accepted in that spirit. Sometimes I would find Dockie upstairs in his photography room with all the lights turned off, except for a flashlight attached to a headband that he wore simply for the fun of it. It was silly stuff, but it was also fun stuff.

Mother and Dockie never really took themselves seriously as grown-ups. This resulted in a feeling we all seemed to share, without even realizing it, that we were all kids together. It never occurred to me that my mother was different because she was more excited about writing poetry than about what the neighbors were doing; or, for that matter, about what might have happened to me during the day. Her attention was so often on other things that we learned early to be quite independent in our own lives. What worked and made the household fun is that we were all crazy about each other, so no matter what the other ones did, it was okay.

I do remember some wonderful free-for-all fights with my sisters, so it cannot be said that it was all goody two-shoes in our life. There was abundant enthusiasm and abundant humor. Other kids, whose parents were far more conventional, found our house a most engaging place to spend time. I have always felt an affinity for the play, "You Can't Take It with You" because 1610 was a perfect replica of that kind of loving, zany living.

Mother's refugee work brought a wonderful family to town, a German family with three boys. The father was a distinguished German lawyer, who had undertaken the defense of an opponent of Hitler who had been falsely accused of a crime. This lawyer paid a high price for serving for the defense. He was sent to jail. After a brief time in prison he managed, along with his family, to escape from Germany and go to England, where they lived for five years before coming to the United States. *Pride and Prejudice's* Mrs. Bennett could not have improved upon the family composition, for the two younger boys in the lawyer's family were just the ages of Pat and me, and the older boy was the same age as Kate.

I remember the first time we met the youngest boy, Jurgen Roetter—the one my age. My sisters and I had planned to rent a rowboat to go out for an afternoon of sunning on nearby Madison's Lake Wingra. We were horrified when Mother told us that she had invited young Jurgen to go with us. "But, Mother," we all cried together, "have you seen our bathing suits? They are almost nonexistent!" Indeed, they were skimpy—perfectly fine for three girls lying in a rowboat with only one another, but not at all respectable for a young lad of tender years.

"Nonsense," replied Mother. "Little German boys are used to swimming in the nude with young girls. This won't be any kind of a problem for him." (She seemed to have mixed things up with Sweden.) In any case, there was nothing we could do except to rather begrudgingly greet him when he arrived for the outing.

And what an outing that was! Young Jurgen (who was, some years later, to become my husband!) found himself with three bathing beauties who perhaps never before, or since, have sunned in such scanty suits. Contrary to Mother's belief, he was not accustomed to nude swimming with women, and that afternoon's frolic in the water gave him a very odd picture of the boating and swimming customs of young women in America. We have laughed many times about that day!

Despite the rather rocky beginning, we were quite thrilled when the Roetter family moved to an apartment just around the corner from 1610. Since Jurgen and I were in the same class, we walked to school together almost every day, and thus, without even knowing it, laid the groundwork for what was to be the best friendship of our lives. At that time, however, it was just fun to have a buddy to walk to school with. How I feel for the children of today, who have to ride the bus, and who therefore miss the charm and variety and good feeling that comes from following the same pathway or walking route to school through the seasons!

Getting back to Wisconsin High School was a real joy after Greenport High. Wisconsin High, the University school, with its mix of career teachers, University professors and student teachers, provided a stimulating and creative atmosphere for its small but bright student body. To give an idea of how energetic and bright the students were, consider the dilemma of finding that there was not enough money in the budget to rent a play for the senior class, and that the problem was solved by the seniors themselves, three of whom wrote, cast, directed, and led rehearsals of their own play. I particularly enjoyed this, because Jurgen and another good friend were the playwrights, and they did not forget me when creating a dramatic role for a female!

What a lot of drama and speech we had at Wisconsin School. Miss Gladys Borchers, a magical person in my memory book, was one of the first women in the country to get a Ph.D. in speech, and we were lucky enough to share her with the University. She had a warmth of manner that made us all eager to perform for her. With what fervor we recited such poems as "Gunga Din" and "The Highwayman" for each other, and for her. What speeches we gave in class, and what declamation contests we entered and often won, because this wonderful woman knew the importance of speech and presentation, and knew how to get us going.

One of our responsibilities was to lead assemblies. We had many of them, and each of us was given the task of standing up in front of the entire student body and leading the assembly at least once during a school term. I remember the day in autumn when it was my turn to lead, and for some reason I couldn't find the assembly hall. I was probably terribly nervous and thus blind to the familiar corridors and doors. In any case, I looked everywhere, and finally walked onto an unknown stage, looked out, and found, to my unutterable amazement, the entire school—teachers and students—seated, waiting for me. "Oh, there you are!" said I. This brought the house down.

Wisconsin High had many clubs. No one knows that better than I, for I not only belonged to five, but was president of four and vice-president of the fifth, all at the same time. Oh, the fun of investigating why the water was warm in the downstairs drinking fountain—one of the tasks of the Student Council, or of planning a dance—one of the responsibilities of our social club! Such busy activities made time interesting and lively in high school. I loved being in the midst of so much action, and I loved the mix of students in the school. I had friends from all groups. We were a bright and intense bunch.

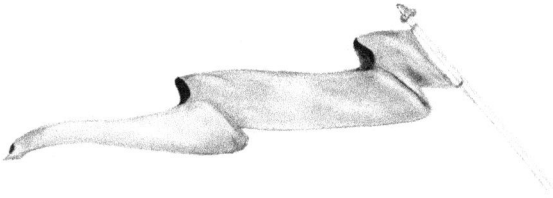

CHAPTER SIX

Nothing in my energetic, busy, bustling years at Wisconsin High prepared me for the shock that lay ahead in my first year in college. Dockie had been invited to teach for a year at Stanford University. Since Stanford offered free tuition to faculty children, this was a great opportunity for us to attend this fine university. I had won a scholarship to the University of Wisconsin, but I gave it up since I was, of course, eager to go to Stanford. I envisioned a splendid year ahead, where I would have more of the same kind of popularity and success I had enjoyed at Wisconsin High. Little did I know.

Mother, Dockie and Kit were to travel to Palo Alto by train, but we children were to drive there with a favorite cousin who had his own car. Kate, Pat, Joel,

Ralph and I were told by our elders to "take our time" on the road since the house we would be renting would not be ready for occupancy before a specific date.

What an assignment that was. We had ten days to drive across the country for the first time in our lives, and to sightsee. This was our first outing without an adult in charge. We felt the great excitement such marvelous independence afforded. High school was behind us; a great college lay ahead, and we had ten days filled with the prairie dogs of the Dakotas, the Rockies, the signs inviting us to Harold's Place in Reno, the tumbling tumbleweeds in Wyoming, the vast plains and antelope of the far West, and then, of course, the great redwoods of California. We sang "California, Here We Come" lustily and in joyous unison every time we crossed a state line. When we finally reached the California state line, we got out of the car, linked arms, and walked across into the magic land singing our song with more volume and vigor than we had ever mustered before.

However, the joy and excitement of getting to California was not matched by what we found when we got there. Stanford was like nothing we had ever experienced. The student body was composed of very rich, bright young Californians for the most part. The Stanford "roughs" wore blue jeans and cashmere sweaters long before they had become the standard garb of the young. These were the days of plaid skirts for girls, and for them too, cashmere sweaters. Not owning a single cashmere was bad enough, but the real barrier and unexpected problem was that of living "at home," which is of course what we did, and it was simply not done. If one did not live on campus in a dorm, one became instantly and automatically known as an "off-campus queer." The prevalent credo on campus was that people did not live away from the dorm unless they were a little strange.

Oh, what agony to suddenly have fallen from my wonderful, exalted position of being a key figure in high school, to that of being not only no one and nothing, but worse, being lumped with all the other "strange ones" who, like us, did not live on campus.

A good example of the kind of snooty attitude

that prevailed at Stanford is illustrated by Kate's experience with her sorority. At Wisconsin, she had been a member of Kappa Kappa Gamma; at Stanford, her Kappa "sisters" requested that she not wear her pin when on campus lest she be confused with one of them. The sorority situation at Stanford was so out of hand, and caused so much pain to so many young women, that within two years of Kate's unhappy encounter, sororities on campus were abolished altogether.

In retrospect, I can see that it was probably good for me to have this shake-up; but oh, what pain it caused at the time! Once more, my two sisters and I were each other's best friends. We used to laugh when we met one another on the campus. Walking along the great and beautiful palisade of trees around the Quad, as it was lovingly known by Stanfordites, we would suddenly spy each other and welcome each other almost with a hug. Suddenly, a lonely walk had turned into a friendly one. Even seeing Professor Salter unexpectedly was a great event. At least one professor knew who we were and paid attention to us!

One very exciting event in that year was taking the course in Western Civilization. It is a wonderful experience to meet the great minds of the world for the first time, and this course gave us that opportunity. I was thrilled to meet the thinkers and philosophers who have shaped our Western thought. Because I had very little social life, I was able to spend a lot of time reading and learning. The same thing was true in the Art History course Kate and I took. Professor Mendelowitz stays in my memory for many reasons, but above all because of his technique of giving us unscheduled tests, something he warned us that he would do, but which in the beginning we didn't take seriously. This proved to be a real stimulus to study and concentrate on a daily basis. We paid attention to each day's assignment, and we learned the subject matter—not just for that one semester, but for life. I have often wondered why more professors don't do the same thing.

I don't know how I would have felt about Stanford if I had lived in a dorm and thus been treated like a "regular" student. It took me a whole year to adjust to the new, isolated, and alienated feelings which living off-campus created. By the end of the school year, I knew I would tackle the whole thing differently if I were to return. I felt ready then to go out for everything, and to not be intimidated by my embarrassment at living off-campus. The test of whether I would have succeeded in all of this, however, was never to come. After that single year, Dockie was going back to Wisconsin. We were therefore no longer tuition-free students. So it was, "So long, Stanford." There were no tears.

The end of our year at Stanford presented a new question. I was nineteen, Pat was twenty, and Kate was twenty-one. It was June, and Dockie had told us that we must support ourselves for the summer. We weren't quite sure as to where to do this, or how. Kit had developed severe asthma earlier in the year, and Mother had moved to Tucson with him before the end of the school year. We considered going to Tucson to join her, but another idea came to us and that had far more appeal. Here we were in California, so why not get a job in this great state?

In fact, thought we, warming to our inspiration, why not go to Hollywood to see whether we could get a job at a movie studio?

This idea electrified us. Three more movie-struck girls than we could scarcely be found in this world. What could be more fun than striking out for the very heart of Southern California where we might find fame and fortune? Talk about visions of sugarplums dancing in one's head. For us, it was visions of being discovered and subsequent stardom that danced in our heads. I had always loved acting, and had read every little account in the movie magazines about people being discovered. Why could it not happen to us?

The thought is mother to the deed, of course. Shortly after school was out, we three were on our way south on the great train which travels between Los Angeles and San Francisco. As good fortune would have it, the same Eva W. whom Mother had befriended in Greenport now had a modest house in Hollywood, so we had a place to stay for a time while we looked for jobs and a dwelling of our own.

To mention Venice, California, at the present is to conjure up the image of a decadent town where anything goes, and most things do. But back in 1943, Venice was a simpler town with a lovely long boardwalk running along the edge of the Pacific Ocean, connecting Venice and Santa Monica. The ocean pounded on the broad sandy beach on one side of the boardwalk, and on the other side there were four- and five-story apartment buildings. Not a fancy spot, but an inviting one. A tramcar ran regularly along the boardwalk providing transportation to various amusements and eating-places. Undeniably, the atmosphere surrounding the whole area was slightly honky-tonk, but we were not disturbed by this. We focused on the joy of being once again right smack at the edge of the sea—and near the glamorous world of Hollywood—at the same time.

We pursued an ad in a local paper that led us to a five-story apartment building on the boardwalk. The landlady looked us over; we looked her over; and then we all looked over a large one-room apartment on the fourth floor. A large room with a closet. Off this room there opened a tiny kitchen that boasted a miniscule counter, one small table, and two chairs. There was of course a bathroom, and this appeared to be all. Where would we sleep, we wondered; whereupon the landlady proudly took us to the closet, opened the door, and out fell a bed! The closet concealed the bed, and of course doubled as a real closet. All belongings that needed to be stored out of sight would go in there. Even though there wasn't actually a great deal of space in the apartment, there was nevertheless a sense of spaciousness, coming probably from the wide open windows through which ocean breezes blew. And the view of the ocean took our breath away. Right outside our window lay the Pacific Ocean. We could see it, and we could hear it, and hearing it was as wonderful and exciting as looking at it. The rent was seventy-five dollars a month, which divided by three would be manageable. There was a cot that could be provided for the third occupant. We decided that nothing stood in our way, and we signed on for our own apartment in Venice, California.

We couldn't believe that we were on our own in this famous and exciting place. The landlady insisted that we call her Mom Matthews. We didn't know then that it was because she liked to stand in as a mother to all of her tenants, and to bombard them with little homilies and maxims and slow-moving tales of her modest adventures. Her slow Southern drawl mesmerized me. When she started talking, whether I wanted to listen or not, I found myself spellbound as she waded through her wearying little anecdotes. I can never hear "Every rose has a thorn," or "Every cloud has a silver lining," without thinking of good old Mom Matthews.

When we rented the apartment, we weren't quite sure what bus we would need to be near, but we learned with glee that the Culver City bus stopped less than five hundred feet from our front door. We wanted a direct line to Culver City because we wanted a job in Culver City's most important industry—the movie business. We aspired to nothing less than employment at Metro-Goldwyn-Mayer.

Our success in finding an apartment on the

ocean had gone to our heads. Why not a job at MGM, we asked ourselves. Why not try to get inside the magic gates? We had learned that the job of messengers, formerly coveted by all Hollywood hopefuls, had fewer applicants now because of the war, and we thought perhaps we might therefore have a chance at being hired. We dressed as neatly and attractively as possible, and set off one morning for an interview at the great studio. We were all overwhelmed with excitement, but for me, there was more. I found that the thrill of actually living in a part of the Hollywood world, on our own, went to my stomach every morning. No matter what I ate, I would throw it up after a meal and then be on my way. This particular morning was no different. I was truly beside myself.

We were interviewed by a man called Bernie—a chunky fellow with eyes that peered at us, and with a breathless air of great self-importance. His tie was thrust around his neck as if he had just raced in from an important engagement. This, we learned later, was a constant condition with Bernie. He looked at us with great interest, smiled in a bemused manner, and quizzed us quite intensely. He wanted to know where we were from, who we were, and why we wanted to be messengers.

We explained that we were three sisters who had been told by their professor-father that they must support themselves now that the Stanford year was over. We explained how fervently we loved the movies, and how much energy and hard work we would bring to the task of being messengers.

And what did it mean to be a messenger at MGM? Simply to deliver messages from point A to point B. To put it more excitingly (and more the way we put it to ourselves) perhaps from Mickey Rooney's dressing room, to Judy Garland's dressing room; or from the stage where Greer Garson was working, to Clark Gable's trailer! One never knew where or who points A and B would be. We knew only that it all took place behind the great Metro-Goldwyn-Mayer gates, and that, miraculously, we were sitting behind those gates, within the confines of MGM right at that very moment!

Incredibly, Bernie hired all three of us right there and then. He cautioned us that he had never before hired sisters, and he was not sure how it would work. We smiled graciously and enthusiastically, to let him see that this was a good decision. He seemed to agree, for he suggested that we all go directly over to Messenger Headquarters where we could meet Evie, the head messenger, see the messenger room, and be introduced to the other messenger girls.

There could scarcely be a less glamorous spot than the messenger room itself: square, brown, three walls lined with benches reminiscent of the bleachers we remembered from high school sports events; and in front of the fourth wall, the large desk where Evie sat and answered the phones.

Evie herself had dyed black shoulder-length hair, heavily made-up eyes and lips, a shrewd suspicious look on her face, and generally a cool and unfriendly manner. The same was true of the several other girls who were assembled. They all viewed us with hostility.

When Bernie presented us by name, and indicated that we were Stanford students, the room temperature fell to a point that would have easily accommodated an ice cube. "College girls, eh?" seemed to be their shared thought. "College girls who think they're better than us, eh? Snobs, eh?" It was clear that our job was not only to learn how to be messengers, but to let these other messengers discover how totally unsnobbish we were. We were all there for the same reason: we needed to support ourselves. The sooner they realized that, the sooner the ice would melt in our headquarters. We were not worried. We were excited; we were friendly too, and we knew that we could thaw things out quickly. Later, we realized how lucky we were that Bernie had decided to take a chance not only on three college girls, but on sisters as well.

Messenger jobs allowed full access to every corner of MGM. The first few days overwhelmed us. Was it possible that we were actually seeing Charles Boyer, Ingrid Bergman, Judy Garland, Dick Powell, and Lucille Ball? And not only seeing them, but delivering messages to them as well? Was that really

Van Johnson who smiled at me as we passed each other on the lot? Did I really see Donald O'Connor rehearsing a dance number when I delivered a message to Stage 4? Was I really sitting next to Marjorie Main on the tram? Who is that looking at me as if his eyes were boring through me? Could it be William Powell giving me that raw, lewd look as I stood waiting to deliver a message to the stage where he was filming?

How impressions poured in on us those first weeks. "And they call this work," we would say to each other. There were two stars who actually liked hanging around the messenger room: Red Skelton, who seemed to need laughter and constant attention, and Mickey Rooney, who was very likeable. Red Skelton was a bit of a strain because he wanted a laugh whether his joke was funny or not.

After a few weeks as a messenger, I was promoted to the commissary during the noon hour, which meant that I stayed in the general dining room during lunch, and took the phones to the stars when they received or made a call. This really enabled me to study these exalted people. There they all were—screenwriters, producers, directors, make-up artists, little stars, big stars—and I could see them all. See them I did, and gradually, ever so gradually, the magic began to wear off.

I was not used to this strange world into which we had catapulted ourselves, a world based on the hierarchy of career and physical appearance. I remember one girl who came to work in the same week with four different hair colors; and the remarkable thing is that no one cared because anything went as far as looks were concerned.

Where one stood on the Hollywood totem pole was determined by how much money one earned, and how one's last movie rated. I had thought I was a lowly being as an "off-campus" student at Stanford. Now I learned what the bottom really was—working as a messenger girl in Hollywood. We had never before judged people by their pocketbook, nor by their status in society. What judging we had done had been on the basis of whether they were interesting or funny or attractive. But now, suddenly,

I was in a world where everybody was considered to be either above or below someone else, and it was this that determined how you were regarded. How people treated you had nothing to do with intrinsic character. You could be an absolute cad and yet be fawned over as if you were a king.

I remember an instance when Marlene Dietrich's make-up assistant was at lunch. A colleague informed her that Miss Dietrich was ready and waiting for her. The make-up worker snorted and said coldly, "Let her wait. I haven't finished my lunch." Marlene's last movie, you see, had flopped, and at the moment she was no longer queen of the lot, so she could jolly well sit and wait for the salaried make-up artist.

I felt as though everything was upside down in Hollywood. Everything I had always believed in seemed in reverse there. As the glamour wore off, different reactions began to emerge, and all began to be somewhat depressing. The famous Hollywood dictum, "The way to the screen is through the casting couch," appeared all too true. Every woman was fair game for some leering eye. The movie magazine stories, filled with tales about the virtues of the stars, appeared to be no more than fabrications. I became increasingly bewildered and disillusioned by the discrepancy between the stars as they really were, and their screen and magazine images.

Nevertheless, to find oneself on a sound stage where a film was being created was to be in the midst of what made Hollywood great. It could be a musical in the works, or a drama. I remember Ingrid Bergman doing "Gaslight," and Greer Garson as Marie Curie. It was said that Miss Garson reached the point where she really believed she had discovered radium. Watching talented, hardworking artists at their craft was indeed a privilege. One became involved, and one realized that this wasn't magic land, but a business, that making movies was hard work, and that movie stars were human beings.

Speaking of stars being human beings brings to mind an amusing story involving Kate. She had struck up a slight, nodding acquaintance with Gene Kelly, one of the most down-to-earth, unspoiled luminaries at MGM. One morning it was her good fortune to get a message for delivery to his dressing room. When she first went over, she found no one there, so she decided that, rather than stick the message under his door, she would hold on to it until later, so that she would have the fun of delivering it to him personally, and perhaps also have a little chat with him.

All day, she made sorties to his dressing room, hoping to deliver the message directly to him. Finally, that evening at six o'clock, she took it over for a last try. By now, all of us in the messenger room were aware of her efforts to put the message into the famous Mr. Kelly's hands, and we waited eagerly for her return. When she finally did come back, her face was beet red with embarrassment. Apparently, she had gone for this last try, and had knocked loudly on the partly open door. When there was no answer, she decided that the only thing to do was to leave the message on the table just inside the room. As she entered carrying the message, there to her great embarrassment, she saw Gene Kelly emerging from the shower with nary a stitch on! They both stopped in their tracks and stared at one another, startled and speechless. Kate dropped the message, then turned and sped from the room. Later, we all quipped that Kate has "seen Gene Kelly all right!" I think, after this episode, there were no more delays in delivering messages. If the star in question wasn't there, we didn't hang around waiting for our heroes or heroines.

One cannot deny that there was a lure to the place. As we wandered over the lot, went to the offices of the talent scouts, or to the directors' bungalows or the writers' building, we felt the call of the dramatic possibilities.

I remember a dramatic woman by the name of Ann Holiday who seemed to take a liking to me. She stopped me once while I was circling the commissary during the lunch hour, and asked me whether I had any dramatic leanings. When I replied that I indeed loved to act, she looked at me musingly, but said nothing. A few days later, she told me that she had made an appointment for me with the director of a little theater group—an actor named Hayden. This sounded good to me because Hayden was my middle name. As it turned out, the name was the only good thing that happened with H. Hayden.

When I arrived for the appointment, I expected to be given something to read, something that would reveal my acting talent. But this was not the case. I entered his office. He sat there, looked at me penetratingly, asked me a few brief questions in a brusque manner, and then explained that there were certain things I would have to do before I could read for a part. He told me, "Cap your teeth, build up your mouth, get a curly halo of hair, and then come back."

I was dumbfounded at this abrupt barrage of suggestions, and amused as well because we were so far from having money for the capping of teeth that the very idea made me laugh. I still laugh. Every now and again, when I feel that I am not looking my best, I say to myself, "Perhaps it's time to cap the teeth, build up the mouth, and get a curly halo of hair." (I have always appreciated my good friend Jurgen's response to Mr. Hayden's suggestions. He stoutly stated that he liked me just exactly the way I was.)

My other attempt to break into Hollywood came when Kate, Pat, and I tried out as a singing trio. Our film friend, Eva W., from Greenport refugee days, insisted that she arrange a singing tryout for us with a director friend of hers. This was the day of singing sisters—the Andrews Sisters, the Lane Sisters; and we thought, "Why not the Salter Sisters?" We were good-looking, so why not? The fact that we were just "back-seat" singers didn't diminish our enthusiasm. We were ready to give it a try. The fact also that Kate didn't ever really sing with us did not discourage us.

Pat and I were convinced we could carry it off, so away we went for the appointment, clad in brilliant red plaid cotton dresses with white ruffles down the front. I can still hear us—three ringing voices—well, perhaps better put, two ringing voices, since Kate was simply mouthing the words, as we offered our spirited, totally unprofessional rendering of "Fascinating Rhythm." It is not that Kate was unwilling to cooperate. It was simply that she was terrified, and such voice as she possessed would not come forth.

We were pretty, we were lively, and we were eager, but we were not singers, so that was the beginning and the end of The Salter Sisters. To this day, however, we have a good laugh over the whole experience, and often when we want to tease Kate after a family song fest, one of us will mention that we "didn't quite hear your voice, Kate!"

We had arrived in Hollywood in June, but by September, we realized that we were a long way from home, and had little money to get us back there. "There" was now Arizona. Kate had enough money to go back to Mills College where she had gone for her freshman year, and to which she had been invited to return on scholarship.

Pat and I were more or less stuck in Hollywood. We tried to figure out a way to leave. I remember walking one morning down the long hallway of the Irving Thalberg Building, the big building at MGM where sat the powerful and the mighty, and saying to a friend who was with me, "I am going to get out of this place!"

As I spoke those words, a nice-looking man who was passing us in the hall stopped and came over to me. He said, "Young lady, will you come into my office? It's all right, my secretary is there. Come in, and tell me why you want to leave."

This was all I needed. I blurted out an account of all my sorrow and disenchantment. I told him how upside down I found things; everything I thought was this way, in Hollywood, turned out to be that way. I said that staying in Hollywood would confuse me, and I might not know the difference between what I used to believe and what Hollywood believed. What I was really saying is that I might lose my soul, and a whole lot more.

He listened attentively, then said to me, "Young lady, you are right. Go away from Hollywood, and don't come back for five hundred years!" He took a piece of paper from his pocket and said, "This is a copy of a telegram I have just sent to my wife in New York City. I've never made so much money in my life as I have since I've been here, but I'm tearing up my contract and going back to New York where life is real. And that's what I told my wife in the telegram. Not only is this place as bad as you say it is; it's worse. Young woman, go!"

It was a memorable talk because this man, a well-known writer, high up in the Hollywood hierarchy, was as disenchanted and unhappy as we were. I do not know what happened to him. But as for us, we took our leave. We left the alleged joys and delights of "tinsel town" behind us forever, and we did so without regret. The only goodbye we had to say that held any real warmth for us was to Mom Matthews, and she made even that tearful scene easier by promising us a "pot of gold at the end of the rainbow," or something comparable. We were on our way now to our own mother and, we hoped, to a restored, normal existence.

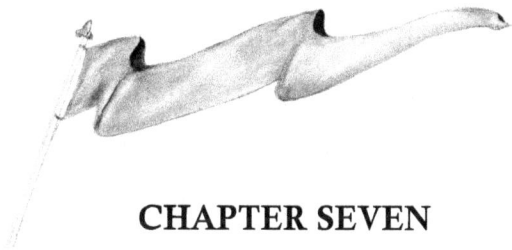

CHAPTER SEVEN

Mother was now in Tucson, Arizona, which turned out to be a wonderfully livable town, not big city-like, but enough city-like to give one the feeling that here was a place where a lot was going on. In addition, there were miles and miles of desert leading to the great Catalina foothills. We became intimately acquainted with the desert that lay on the outskirts of Tucson because, thanks to Granddad, Mother had purchased a small house on an acre of land in the desert in the shadow of the foothills.

The house was absolutely simple—primitive even. The shower was outside the house, nestled in the middle of morning glory vines; and until later when we had work done by a skillful, inexpensive plumber, there was no indoor plumbing. It was quite enchanting to step out for a shower and have your own private leafy vine as a curtain. Less so, to step outside at all hours, including the middle of the night, to the distant outhouse! In any case, it was our new home, and we were overjoyed to be there.

The house was made of adobe, and the walls were painted white. There was a large living room, and a fine sleeping porch from which we could view the vast Arizona sky with its magic display of stars, or watch the slow transformation of the sky at sunset from blue to a wash of colors, which turned the sky into a mighty painter's palette. The Arizona sky was somehow different from any other sky we had ever seen. It is so large, and so beautiful, that it deserves a name of its own. I remember us, night after night, at twilight "Ohh'ing" and "Ahh'ing" at the sunsets, until Mother said we would all have sore throats if we kept this up!

When I first saw the desert, I felt it was arid and barren, but what a wonderful change of perception takes place as you live in that world. I discovered that it was infinitely alive, teeming with plants and living creatures, flowers and grasses—all vivid, and all marvelously adapted to the heat and the parched earth that characterize the desert.

Also adapted to the desert and its demands were some of Mother's excellent new friends, with whom we became acquainted as soon as we settled in. She had been put in touch with a long-time Tucson family by the name of Griffiths, and it is with these people, Vic and "Gaga," that she and Kit stayed until they could move into their own little house. The Griffiths were both in their seventies, and they had a Walter Brennan quality about them—real Western characters, full of the flavor of mesquite and saguaro cactus. Vic told tales about the early days in Tucson—about Indians and covered wagons, coyote and wild boar, rattlesnakes and tarantulas, hardworking women, men who were men—the sort of tales that we lovers of movies could not fail to appreciate.

Their large, rambling house was at the edge of town. A spacious porch ran across the entire front of the house. It was there that we sat for many a lazy hour listening to Vic's tales of old Arizona.

But even more exciting than meeting Vic and Gaga was meeting a truly great woman, Margaret Sanger. Earlier, Mother's writings had led her into correspondence with Margaret and they discovered that they shared many thoughts and ideas. When Kit developed serious asthma in Palo Alto, it was Margaret who suggested that Mother bring him to Tucson (where she herself lived at the time), and it was she who found the Griffiths for Mother and Kit. Our first encounter with her was particularly lovely, and Pat and I were properly dazzled.

Shortly after our arrival in Tucson, Margaret appeared, in company with her invaluable assistant/helper, David, and announced that she had brought dinner, which David would prepare. We all sat and talked and ate, and enjoyed the intimate and delightful experience of dining out—in our own home.

Margaret Sanger was fun! She had a great penchant for making each moment as nice as it could be. You didn't waste time waiting for a good time, you made a good time. She was a very pretty woman, feminine, bright, extremely "modern." I remember telling her that I didn't know how to drive. She replied, "You must learn how to drive, Jean. You should not only know how to drive, you should also learn how to fly an airplane. That's what your world calls for. I wish I could learn to fly." I was impressed by her vigorous response, and I have never forgotten it. I have learned to drive, but flying still lies ahead. One got straight talk from Margaret Sanger—no false sympathy, no pulling of punches. She found solutions to problems, and expected you to do the same.

Because Mother and Margaret had become such good friends, we had the benefit of her friendship, as well. I shall always prize the memory of my twentieth birthday. Margaret herself was hostess for the occasion, and once again the remarkable and wonderful David arrived, laden with a basket of delectable goodies.

Margaret, Mother, Pat, and two of our new Tucson friends sallied forth for an all-day picnic at Sabino Canyon, one of the scenic delights of the Tucson area. It was a lazy and lovely day.

I found myself very interested in the politics of the young guests. It was my first encounter with wealthy youth who espoused the cause of Communism. Louise R. was quite rabid on the subject. I was puzzled because I knew that her family had made their fortune in the bottling industry, and I wondered why she would want to see Communism erase all of this. Since that time I have seen many young people support causes which would result in the overthrow of their family fortunes. Often these ardent young folk do their demonstrating from the security of private college campuses. It has occurred to me that if they really objected to wealth, they would do well to divest themselves of its trappings, thus giving more substance to their demonstrations.

One of the things we loved about Margaret Sanger was her femininity. She in no way emulated men. She was as strong as any man, but she derived her strength by productivity, using all of her own native powers to accomplish her ends, and not by dressing like a man, or trying to conduct herself like a man. She was an inspiration to me because she did so much, and yet never lost herself in what she was doing.

The Arizona air worked its beneficence on Kit almost as soon as he arrived. He grew strong and healthy. Mother, on the other hand, was physically— to use her own words—"a wreck." She was plagued by intense internal discomfort, the result it seemed of what was fashionably called "female problems." It looked as though some sort of corrective surgery would have to be done, and who would do it and where it would be done became the important questions of the day. Little did I realize what an impact all of this was going to have on my life.

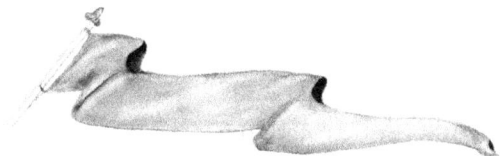

CHAPTER EIGHT

Pat had returned to Wisconsin, where Dockie was once more teaching. Joel again, thanks to Granddad, was attending our uncle's school, Western Reserve Academy in Cleveland, Ohio. So Mother and I were left alone in the desert with five-year-old Kit. I was a little restless, but it seemed all right until I got the drift of a plan hatching in Mother's head. She had a cousin who was a successful doctor in New York City. Applying the same logic that had taken us to all the different spots we had moved to and lived in, Mother decided that no one could operate on her as well as Cousin Charlie Fitch. Eagerly, she devised a plan that would take her to New York for the operation, and leave me in Arizona to take care of Kit.

The plan had no more been conceived than it was acted on. Before I knew fully what was happening, I found myself living alone on the desert with my little brother. What a time that was. What a feeling, to wake up in the morning and know that my brother and I had the whole day ahead, with very little going on to break the daily routine of quiet living on the vast and mysterious desert.

It was then that I learned how important it is to have a little grit in life. Never before had I had all the time I wanted for reading books; but now that I had the needed time, I didn't want to read. Because I had no impediment to make me struggle a little to find the reading time, I didn't have any interest. It is that little struggle which I call grit; and for me, there has to be a little of it in daily life. I found a couplet in a book that perfectly characterized my feelings and I made it my slogan.

> "Many a flower is born to blush unseen
> and waste its fragrance on the desert air."

Along with the solitariness of our present desert life came a new element—the financial one, which certainly did no credit to Dockie. He simply stopped sending me money. I knew it was because he didn't have any money, but that didn't help me when it came time to pay the electric bill.

It was then that my good friend Margaret Sanger brought her practical mind to the rescue. "What you need, Jean is a job. You can make money. You can get out, and Kit can go to a nursery school." She did more than simply suggest; she lent me the money for the first month of nursery school, and thus enabled me to leave my desert roost.

Davis Monthan's B-29 factory was just outside of Tucson, and they were hiring. They were looking for people to string communication wires within the planes, and they hired me for the job. What excitement I felt as I suddenly found myself with a tool kit in my hands, a visor-cap on my head, and a time clock to check in on at seven in the morning.

There was not much talk of self-image in the '40s, and I cannot remember having given much thought to the matter. But certainly, if there was one image I had never carried of myself, it was that of being a mechanic on a giant airplane. Every time I picked up a piece of wire and started stringing it, I had to pinch myself to be sure it was really me. It was exciting to be part, not only of the outside world again, but also of the war effort. Many of my friends were in the service now, and to be so removed from all war effort was not my choice.

Kit and I did our war stint together for four months. He did his part adorably by cheerfully going to nursery school. I always had to leave a little ahead of him, but he accepted this and was a very cooperative little brother. As for me, I had joined a car pool that arrived every morning at six-thirty and except for the fact that my fellow back seat driver smelled as if he spent every night eating garlic and drinking whiskey, all went very well.

This was a little pocket of time unlike any other moment in my life. I was alone, without my sisters, older brother or parents. I was independent and I was doing a job that was completely out of character, but was stimulating. I enjoyed that time.

There were two times in that period when we might have had some danger come to us, but happily we didn't even know it when it was happening. One night, as I lay asleep in my bed on the screened-in porch, I was jarred from my sleep by a horrible caterwauling. I opened my eyes and discovered at least six big wild desert cats clawing and climbing up on the screens of the porch. They had converged on this porch and wanted to get in. All I felt at that time was indignation that they were interrupting my night's sleep. I must have been very groggy as I punched the screen and told them loudly to "Get Going!" I wasn't afraid of them, only annoyed. It was all I could do to get rid of them, but I did, then managed to get back to sleep. In the morning I felt as though it must have been a dream since it seemed so weird and unlikely that the desert cats would find their way to my porch. They never came again, but it was like a nightmare waking up and finding them there.

Another uninvited critter was a tarantula that comfortably found a spot on our door. I attacked it with a broom and was once more victorious. Either of these things happening now would leave me a fearful chicken, but being young and sassy, I was also young and bold, and it was just part of the Tucson day.

June 6, 1944 was D-Day for the world, and it was also D-Day for Kit and me. It was the day of our departure from Tucson. Two train tickets had materialized from some family member, and we found ourselves saying goodbye to our good friends, and to our little desert home. I had learned to love the desert, but I was glad to be leaving it at last. One feels very small in comparison to the giant natural phenomenon that is a desert, with all of its magic, teaming life, and ever-changing foothills. One feels almost that it will seize you and hold you forever in its spell. I didn't want this to happen to Kit and me. It was good that we were on our way back to 1610.

Being back at 1610 was different from what it had been a year earlier, when we had prepared to leave for Stanford and the great California adventure. Although we were all together again, except for Kate who was still at Mills College, things were not the same. For one thing, we had to make our own way, and earn our own money. Only Kit and Joel were considered dependents. Pat and I had to find jobs in Madison that would give us enough to save towards our college in the fall.

Mother was very busy with her letter-writing activities. By now, we could hardly get her attention, much less keep it for any length of time. Her mind was on world concerns, and she gave little time or energy to us. Dockie was glad enough to have us back, and dear Granddad had decided to join forces permanently with us, so we had him now as a regular new resident. So we were all once more living together at 1610, but our customary élan and delight were lacking. Everything seemed more serious and difficult, and less joyous.

There was only one place where we could make a decent salary as unskilled laborers, and that was at the Oscar Mayer meat packing plant. You never think of yourself as an unskilled laborer until someone asks you what you do, and then you learn quickly enough that you really don't do anything. Pat and I both realized this about ourselves that summer, so we were glad to get a job at Oscar Mayer.

If you lived on the east side of town and simply followed your nose, you could find Oscar Mayer's easily—its strong odor announced its location in the neighborhood. Happily for us, we lived on the west side. We did have to take a very early morning bus, however, for our shift started at six o'clock. We were at the bus stop by five-fifteen!

Talk about self-image—what a change! I had to do some fast adjusting to come to terms with being a packer in a meatpacking factory. And here, as in the messenger room at MGM, we had to contend with instant hostility from the regular workers who didn't like college kids coming in. They suspected that we thought we were better than they were. More importantly, they feared that we might be faster on the production line and that would raise the expectations of their bosses.

We didn't feel superior to them, but we surely felt different. It was such a totally new world for us—punching a time clock at six in the morning, making our way to the picnic butt packing line, and then standing in one spot for hours on end, wrapping saran wrap about the butts as they moved down the assembly line. It was deadly work—monotonous and repetitious. Time barely moved.

Unexpected interruptions were frowned on. I remember being told by one person in authority, when I needed to use the restroom, that if I had been trained properly as a child, I wouldn't have to leave until break time. Only our sense of humor pulled us through. Although I cannot remember a single example of wit or cleverness from the other employees, I vividly remember that many of us— particularly the temporary workers—were often in gales of laughter (when we could get away with it), and that we grew more clever by the day. Better to laugh than scream was our philosophy.

Pat and I were nearly always side by side. But on one occasion, I was dispatched to do a different task. I was assigned to a room upstairs where slab bacon was processed. My job was to stand in a boiling hot room where there were great hunks of bacon hanging on a revolving rack, and to flick off any sort of impurities or imperfect particles that I spotted with a huge fork-like implement. Again, the time went infinitely slowly.

What a feeling of release one had at the end of the workday. The pleasure of stepping into the outside world again, where the air smelled sweet and people pursued tasks other than wrapping animal flesh, was unalloyed. I valued time off beyond all things, and I learned to value the fact that I was working to put together money for college. I could see my options very clearly now. I could see that if I didn't get an education, I would be forever stuck and have no control over what I did, because I would have to settle for what was available. I would not be able to pick and choose. So I was powerfully motivated, and I am sure that is what made working at Oscar's endurable.

That was an intense summer. In the world itself, there was the drama of our new life, working in a giant meat packing plant that was playing itself out day by day. At the same time, another drama began playing out in our lives. Granddad became ill with prostate cancer. He had treated it sensibly but lightly, and we all thought it could be easily taken care of.

Alas, we were wrong. Granddad did not get better. At first, he was able to stay at home, and we would rush into his room at the end of our workday, to talk with him, to sing to him, to play his beloved cards with him. But his condition deteriorated, and the hospital became necessary.

Pat and I rode the bus to the hospital every day to visit him. The sweetness of his nature never changed, even as he grew more ill. We would find him lying patiently in his bed, his cheeks no longer pink, and his eyes less merry. When we would tell him, as we repeatedly did, that "We miss you, Granddad," he would smile and say, with almost a sigh, "It's nice to be missed." His thoughts were always of the family, and, I imagine, of how we would manage without him.

He had given us all such stability and love that it was as if he had been a warm stove in our lives. We had taken this from him, and not thought a lot about it. But now, as the reality of his condition became clear, we were overwhelmed by the realization of how infinitely important he was to us.

Mother spent her days at the hospital. Pat and I came each day, and I remember crying my way home on the bus, day after day. I had never experienced the death of someone I loved, and it was terribly hard. Pat and I were wrapped in grief by night, as we wrapped bacon and ham by day.

As the end approached, his mind wandered, but not totally. The last time I saw him, he talked of teamwork, and of how vital it was for the success of anything. He talked to us because he worried about us. After this last visit with him, I came home and reported to Mother that he seemed all right, although very weak. But Mother, even though she had spent the entire day at the hospital, somehow chose to go back. When she reached his bedside, he was moaning and making anxious little sighing sounds. Mother began singing hymns in her lovely contralto voice, and Granddad grew quiet. She held his hand as he slipped away.

And then Granddad was gone. His death was a powerful moment in the life of our family. We did not know at the time how powerful. We knew that we had lost someone very dear and precious to us, but we didn't realize that we had also lost a force that had been like ballast to our little ship, a center that held us together. Mother's new passion for political writing had been somewhat contained by the presence of her beloved father. But now that he was gone, she was unrestrained in her involvement with her beliefs, with her political convictions, with her persistent writing.

Within weeks of Granddad's death, Mother had decided to engage a printing company to produce a book of her materials. She had amassed hundreds of her "Letters to the Editor," and these she proposed to draw together into one volume which would be, in her opinion, a brilliant and lucid indication of the times—of the sentiments of the public, of the political atmosphere of our world. Although no publisher was in sight at that time, she had raised quite a sum of money from the various affluent and intelligent people with whom she corresponded, and who supported her views and applauded her work.

Without further ado, she packed up her typewriter, her personal belongings, and her loyal little son Kit, bade us goodbye, and went off to Oberlin, Ohio— there to stay until the book was completed.

At almost the same time, Dockie was offered the unlikely job of writing a history of the United States Air Force, a job for which he seemed scarcely qualified, but which nevertheless he accepted with delight, if for no other reason than that it took him to Washington DC, a city which he loved.

So suddenly, Joel, Pat, and I found ourselves without parents, without visible means of support, and, since 1610 was part of Granddad's estate and would therefore need to be sold, without even a roof over our heads! We found that Granddad's death seemed to act as a catalyst for the growing up of our family—and as well for its permanent elimination as a single living unit. We never again lived as a family under one roof.

Pat and I found ourselves in charge of the whole process of seeing the contents of 1610 leave for Oberlin, Ohio in the moving van. When the moving men came, several hours late, we stood in the cold and empty shell of 1610. Everything had been boxed up, ready for the van. But as we waited, we had a chance to feel, for the last time, the wonderful vibrations that had made us all so happy in that Madison home, 1610.

We knew that, in leaving 1610, one phase of our lives was forever gone. But, full of the invincible spirit that Mother and Granddad had so marvelously epitomized to us, we also knew that other wonderful things lay ahead. We were ready for the change. We were eager to see what was, as Mother had so often promised, just around the corner!